Coaching Skills for

Helping Others Reach Their Potential

Sam R. Lloyd
Tina Berthelot

A Crisp Fifty-Minute™ Series Book

Coaching Skills for Leaders
Helping Others Reach Their Potential

Sam R. Lloyd
Tina Berthelot

CREDITS:

Product Manager:	**Debbie Woodbury**
Editor:	**Ann Gosch**
Production Editor:	**Genevieve McDermott**
Production Artists:	**Nicole Phillips, Rich Lehl, and Betty Hopkins**

Trademarks

Crisp Series is a trademark of Axzo Press.

Some of the product names and company names used in this book have been used for identification purposes only and may be trademarks or registered trademarks of their respective manufacturers and sellers.

Disclaimer

We reserves the right to revise this publication and make changes from time to time in its content without notice.

ISBN 10: 1-4188-6492-7
ISBN 13: 978-1-4188-6492-7
Library of Congress Catalog Card Number 2005936330
Printed in the United States of America
3 4 5 6 09 08

Learning Objectives for

COACHING SKILLS FOR LEADERS

The learning objectives for *Coaching Skills for Leaders* are listed below. They have been developed to guide the user to the core issues covered in this book.

The objectives of this book are to help the user:

1) Gain skill and confidence in observing those who are going to be coached

2) Establish rapport as a prelude to giving effective feedback

3) Use learning styles to improve training abilities

4) Learn and practice active listening techniques

5) Coach others to solve their own problems

Assessing Progress

A Crisp Series **assessment** is available for this book. The 25-item, multiple-choice and true/false questionnaire allows the reader to evaluate his or her comprehension of the subject matter.

To download the assessment and answer key, go to www.courseilt.com and search on the book title.

Assessments should not be used in any employee-selection process.

About the Authors

Sam R. Lloyd is president and founder of SuccessSystems, Inc. in Boulder, Colorado. The company has been a provider of training and coaching services for organizations and individuals since 1977. Sam is the author of five other books and numerous articles.

Before starting SuccessSystems, Sam was the director of the Management Development Center for the Cox School of Business at Southern Methodist University. Earlier in his career, he was assistant dean for Continuing Education in the School of Business Administration at the University of Missouri-St. Louis.

Sam is the past president of the Rocky Mountain Chapter of the American Society for Training & Development (ASTD) and is on the board of the Boulder Area Human Resources Association, a chapter of the Society for Human Resource Management (SHRM).

Tina Berthelot is vice president and owner of SuccessSystems. Before joining the company in 1983, she was a stockbroker for several years and earlier worked in human resources with International Harvester. She is the author of two other books and several articles.

Tina is a member of the Boulder Area Human Resources Association, the Colorado Human Resources Association, and the Society for Human Resource Management (SHRM). She was a program co-chair for the 2005 Colorado State Human Resources Conference and is the northern chapter relations director for the Colorado State SHRM Council.

SuccessSystems, Inc. is an approved provider of recertification credits for the PHR/SPHR/GPHR certifications granted by SHRM and the HR Certification Institute. You may contact Sam and Tina at (303) 998-0248 or succsyst@peakpeak.com. The company Web site is www.trainingforsuccess.com.

Preface

Why has so much attention been focused on coaching in recent years? An important reason is the continuing need for performance management in organizations of all kinds. With global competition increasing the pressure to improve productivity with lower costs, managers are seeking to enhance their skills for working with people to get the best results possible.

Another reason is the growing awareness that younger generations have different expectations than did previous generations. They expect to have more opportunity for personal growth, rapid career advancement, a more balanced life, and leaders who will help them achieve these goals. If they do not get what they want, they are quick to go elsewhere to get their needs met.

In this book you will learn tools and techniques that, with practice, will become important skills to help you work with younger employees and seasoned veterans to help them work as productively as possible and be the best they can be inside or outside the workplace. Although this book focuses on coaching for performance management, its use need not be limited to the workplace. You may apply many of these skills to coaching your children, people you lead in community activities, aspiring professionals seeking career mentoring, or peers and friends desiring counsel on personal matters.

You will learn how to give both positive and negative feedback skillfully to help people improve performance, learn new skills, hone existing skills, and develop into leaders. You will learn how to help people learn from their mistakes and develop more confidence with risk-taking, how to use your feedback skills to reinforce desirable behaviors and reduce people's need for using undesirable behaviors to get attention, how to meet the motivational needs of different types of people, and how to caringly confront those problem behaviors that do appear from time to time.

Learning is an active process so the more you work your way through this book, the more you will gain from it. You will get the most from the book by doing all of the exercises.

Sound like a lot of work? Being a leader has always been a lot of work, but when you become a coach/leader you will find that the work is more rewarding. Helping others learn, grow, and develop is rewarding for you and is greatly appreciated by those you help. Your organization will benefit, too, because your employees will have stronger loyalty, higher motivation, and greater commitment. They will be more accountable and will remember you as a positive influence in their lives.

Ready to get started? Let's start learning.

Sam Lloyd and Tina Berthelot

What Is Coaching?

"Building awareness, responsibility, and self-belief is the goal of a coach."

–John Whitmore, *Coaching for Performance*

You probably have some ideas about what coaching is and you are likely a leader of some sort because you are reading this book. So let's get at what coaching is by defining some terms.

What is your definition of a manager?

_____

_____

The answers to this question most often include the following—someone who:

- ➤ Provides direction for others
- ➤ Sets goals and makes plans
- ➤ Oversees the work
- ➤ Allocates resources
- ➤ Solves problems

Management textbooks typically define *manager* as "someone who gets things done through others."

Managers do all of the above things and the textbook definition is pretty good. Some supervisors work side by side with employees doing some of the work; but most often, supervisors and managers are responsible for making sure that employees do the various kinds of work that must be done to accomplish the goals of the organization.

What is your definition of a leader?

_____

_____

Coaching Skills for Leaders

The answers to this question most often describe someone who:

- ➤ Inspires others with vision
- ➤ Takes risks
- ➤ Makes decisions confidently
- ➤ Delegates and uses the skills of others effectively
- ➤ Communicates well

When you stop to think about it, a leader is simply someone whom others choose to follow. Why others choose to follow can be those things listed above or other qualities such as charisma or political connections. Developing coaching skills will help supervisors and managers become better leaders. People will trust you, will have more confidence in you, and will have much stronger loyalty when you become their coach.

What is your definition of a coach?

_____

_____

This question often elicits similar answers but also some different ones. People say that coaches:

- ➤ Teach others what to do and how to do it
- ➤ Inspire or motivate people to do their best
- ➤ Provide encouragement and moral support
- ➤ Give lots of feedback to help improve skills
- ➤ Urge people to continue improving
- ➤ Confront when the person is doing the wrong thing

Did you have similar responses when you answered the questions? You could think of coaching as helping someone be all they can be.

What skills do coaches use to help others continue doing what they do well, to improve in those areas where they can do better, to correct what they are doing poorly, and to continue learning and striving for excellence? Write what skills would be needed in the spaces below:

1. _____
2. _____
3. _____
4. _____
5. _____
6. _____

Did you list six skills? Does your list also include some personality attributes? It is sometimes difficult to separate *skills*—behaviors that have been developed to a high level of proficiency—and *attributes* such as intuition, creativity, and empathy. No matter. Even these attributes can be developed to some extent by learning new behaviors and practicing them.

Here are the skills most important for successful coaching:

➤ Observing behavior

➤ Giving feedback

➤ Teaching

➤ Asking the right questions at the right time

➤ Listening

➤ Facilitating problem solving

➤ Confronting

➤ Supporting and encouraging

More and more organizations are encouraging managers to learn coaching skills because when managers start thinking of themselves as coaches, their whole mind-set changes. When you learn to be a coach, you will shift your expectations. You will find yourself looking for ways to help people improve instead of waiting for them to mess up and create a problem that you have to fix. This change in your perspective will be communicated to those you lead, and their perception of you will change favorably too.

Table of Contents

Observing

Behavior as a

Prelude to

Coaching

> " *To coach the people who work for you, you must know what the behavior is now, so you are able to recognize whether your coaching is helping.*"

–paraphrase of Ferdinand F. Fournies,
Coaching for Improved Work Performance

Managing by Walking Around

Most supervisors and managers do not follow the practice of MBWA—Managing by Walking Around—and they fail to notice what could be improved. They also miss opportunities to reinforce what is being done well. Being a good observer is an acquired skill.

Even experienced professional athletic coaches do not see every little thing that needs improvement. This is why they often use video recordings and replays to help pinpoint the behaviors that need to be changed. Even a slight change in the swing of a golfer or baseball batter can make a significant difference in the results.

Concerns About Observing Behavior

Many supervisors and managers have concerns that keep them from Managing by Walking Around and observing their employees in ways that would help them be better coaches. Common concerns are listed below. Check (√) any that might apply to you.

- ❑ Employees will think that I don't trust them.

- ❑ People don't like others looking over their shoulder.

- ❑ It would take time away from other responsibilities.

- ❑ Employees would think that I don't have enough to do.

- ❑ My boss does not approve of my spending too much time with employees.

- ❑ I am uncomfortable about spying on people.

- ❑ I feel awkward about just observing and don't know what to say.

The next sections address these concerns and provide suggestions for rethinking each one.

Fostering Mutual Trust and Respect

Avoiding the appearance of suspicion of your employees is a legitimate concern. To be an effective coach you must have a relationship built on mutual trust and respect.

Which of the ideas below would work for you to be able to observe your employees without eroding trust? Check (√) all that you think might be effective.

❑ Have a meeting with all employees to tell them that I have decided to pay more attention to what they do so I can provide more helpful performance evaluations.

❑ Send an e-mail message to all employees to inform them that I have decided to pay more attention to what they do so I can provide more helpful performance evaluations.

❑ Tell each employee individually that I have decided to pay more attention to what they do so I can provide more helpful performance evaluations.

❑ Start visiting the work area to ask how things are going, comment on what the employees are doing, ask how I can help and gradually increase the number of times that I do it.

❑ During each employee's next performance appraisal tell them that I plan to do a better job with their next evaluation and will be making a special effort to observe them more often to help me do that.

Any of these ideas might work and it is important that you use the one that fits best for you and your workplace. The more personal approach is usually preferable to an e-mail message. E-mail is often interpreted by the reader in a more negative manner than you intended. Even if that does not occur, e-mail is very likely to feel impersonal and uninvolved to employees compared to in-person interaction. Be sure to let people know why you will be around more often; don't just start showing up. The idea of gradually being around more could certainly work if you sincerely demonstrate interest in what your employees are doing.

When your employees know that you are there to help them and to carry out your responsibilities, they will not see you as a "spy." When you become more skilled at listening effectively and giving positive feedback, any concern you may have had about not knowing what to say will lessen. When your employees start receiving more frequent positive feedback from you, they will be less likely to be uncomfortable with your observing their work. And they will be pleased that you are paying more attention.

What are some things you could do in your workplace to help your employees feel comfortable with your being there while they work?

_____

_____

_____

_____

Deeming Observation as Part of Your Job

Being uncomfortable with "spying" on people is a virtue to be admired. All that may be necessary to overcome this barrier to observing employees is to redefine what you are doing. Because you are responsible and accountable for performance and improving productivity, you are simply doing your job when you observe your employees.

One of the most common challenges in increasing the amount of time you spend observing your employees is managing your time to make sure that you carry out all of your job responsibilities. But remember that one of the most important responsibilities of all managers is ensuring that employees do their work as well as it can be done.

In the following table, list the results you are responsible for producing.

Results to Be Achieved	Rank	Hours

Now rank the different results and responsibilities by importance. Be sure that you evaluate them for how important each is to your organization, to your manager, and to your own goals and not according to urgency. Sometimes others are in a hurry for you to get something done that might not be as important as other things you need to accomplish.

Next, estimate how much time is required each week to accomplish the most important results by the time limit.

Assuming that you have ranked performance management as one of your important results and that you are aware that you must allot some time to observing employees, your next step will be to figure out how to use your time effectively and efficiently. Delegating some responsibilities to others will free up some time.

Allaying Other Concerns About Observing

Some leaders are concerned that if they start spending more time with employees in the work area, employees might get the impression that the leader does not have enough to do. But the alternatives presented earlier about communicating your reason for being there should take care of that concern.

You might also want to consider sharing with employees all of your responsibilities and the results you hope to achieve. When doing that, emphasize the importance of your being responsible for helping them do their jobs as well as they can and that you hope to do a better job with that responsibility.

Seeking Support from Your Own Manager

If your own manager disapproves of your spending much time with employees, that will be a major obstacle for your being an effective coach. What can you do to influence a change in your manager's perspective?

_____

_____

_____

_____

Consider these additional options:

➤ Arrange a meeting with your manager to discuss your responsibilities and the expectations for your performance. During that discussion you can raise your concern about doing a better job of coaching your employees to help them improve their performance and ask your manager for agreement on this priority.

➤ Prepare data to present to your manager to demonstrate how your coaching efforts have resulted in some cost savings, productivity gains, fewer absences, and the like. Compare *before* and *after* figures to show how your spending more time with employees has made a difference.

What to Look for in Your Observations

The purpose of observing employees is to look for the behaviors that are related to the work they have been assigned to do. Even though this may sound easy to do, it will probably take some practice.

An important first step is to prepare a list of the behaviors to watch. With each job that you supervise, identify what behaviors are required to produce the desired results.

You may want to create a description as in the example below for each job to help you pinpoint what to observe.

JOB: Technical Writer

COMPETENCIES REQUIRED:

➤ Writing skills (composition, grammar, clarity)

➤ Time management skills (meeting deadlines)

➤ Communication skills (asking questions of subject matter experts, listening, translating jargon into plain language for readers)

➤ Computer skills (skillful use of Microsoft Word, Excel, Publisher, internal Web site resources)

➤ Interpersonal skills (rapport with co-workers, subject matter experts, manager, accepting feedback skillfully)

➤ Stress management skills (handling time pressure, staying healthy)

While this idea is fresh in your mind, pick one of the jobs that you supervise and practice identifying the competencies required and the behaviors to observe.

JOB: _____

COMPETENCIES REQUIRED:

_____

_____

_____

_____

_____

If this is an existing job, ask the employees who are doing it to help you identify the competencies required for the job.

Most jobs involve many more competencies and behaviors than we realize until we start examining them to identify everything that is required to do the job well. This process will not only help you know what to observe, it will also identify areas where you can help someone improve with more training or coaching from you.

CASE STUDY: Each Learns from Observation

Rachel was a dependable call center representative who had never arrived late for work or taken extended breaks, consistently completed calls within the standard, and had very few complaints from customers.

Jahnavi, the supervisor, was thinking about Rachel in preparation for completing a performance appraisal the following month. Even though Rachel's performance was acceptable and she had caused no problems, Jahnavi had a nagging feeling that she was capable of more and decided to observe her more carefully for a while.

During the next week Jahnavi started walking through the call center more frequently than usual and stopped to chat briefly with different employees when they were not busy with a call. During these visits to the call center she made an extra effort to observe Rachel and other employees.

Jahnavi noticed that the call center representatives would complete a call and immediately make notes in their call logs. When chatting with the reps, Jahnavi looked at their notes and saw that often they had written not only what the problem was and how it had been resolved, but they also had made a suggestion about how to prevent the problem from recurring.

Jahnavi realized that she could not recall ever seeing suggestions on Rachel's call logs and checked her reports from the past few months. The check confirmed that Rachel had made no suggestions.

Jahnavi decided to discuss this with Rachel during the performance evaluation meeting and suggest to her that making suggestions about the customer service situations she handled would increase her chances for bonuses. When Jahnavi mentioned this, she was surprised when Rachel responded, "I have thought about doing that several times but I was afraid you would think I was sticking my nose into your business."

CONTINUED

Jahnavi explained to Rachel that she would appreciate receiving all of the suggestions Rachel could offer. Rachel seemed excited about that possibility and submitted several suggestions the next day. She continued to include suggestions each week.

1. What benefit(s) did Jahnavi derive from observing her call center employees?

   _____

   _____

   _____

2. How was Rachel helped by Jahnavi's observations?

   _____

   _____

   _____

3. What potential benefit to the company could result?

   _____

   _____

   _____

Compare your answers to the authors' suggested responses in the Appendix.

P A R T 2

Giving Effective

Feedback

The Human Need for Attention

Why is feedback so powerful? All human beings are born with a need for attention and we never seem to get enough. Much like food provides fuel for our bodies to operate, attention is a source of emotional and psychological energy that feeds our abilities for thinking, feeling, and behaving. We all need to know that who we are and what we do matters to others. Coaching is a demonstration that someone is aware and that someone cares.

All types of attention reinforce whatever prompted the attention. When we do something that results in our getting attention, we are very likely to do the same thing again. What many people do not realize is that negative attention works just like positive attention. All forms of attention can reinforce the behavior that resulted in getting the attention.

This powerful effect of attention is magnified when the person giving attention is a significant person. That is one reason for supervisors and managers to become coaches. When you ignore employees' good performance, you inadvertently encourage them to seek negative attention. When you give employees attention only when they do a poor job, you run the risk of undermining their confidence and loyalty. You also may be giving them a reason to continue their poor work.

Negative Attention Is Better Than No Attention

When people do not get enough positive attention, they resort to negative behaviors so they will get at least some kind of attention. Behaviors that are often used to get attention on the job include the following:

- ➤ Make a lot of mistakes
- ➤ Come to work late quite often
- ➤ Complain frequently
- ➤ Talk a lot about personal problems (finances, children, spouse, car, etc.)
- ➤ Entertain others with jokes, funny stories, pranks
- ➤ Get sick frequently
- ➤ Make negative comments in meetings
- ➤ Blame others when things go wrong

Some people have been using such behaviors since they were children—because they work. People do give attention to such behaviors and even though it might not be positive attention, almost any kind of attention is better than none at all.

When people start receiving positive attention more frequently, the undesirable behaviors often disappear. They may not disappear completely if someone learned to use the behaviors as a child—they have had many years of practice and changing old patterns of behavior is difficult.

CASE STUDY: Seeking Attention from the Boss

Paul was a very good salesman. He had loyal customers who purchased more on average than did the customers of the other salespeople.

He was friendly and charming with customers and the other sales personnel, but he usually ignored the administrative staff when he was in the headquarters office. The only time Paul ever visited the warehouse was when there had been a late shipment to one of his customers. Even though this happened rarely, when one of his customers complained about a late shipment, Paul would go to the warehouse to talk with Victor, the shipping manager.

Victor would explain the reason for the delayed shipment and apologize to Paul for the inconvenience to his customer, but Paul would angrily accuse Victor of being a poor manager who did not care about customer service. Lately the number of late shipments to Paul's customers seemed to be increasing.

Veronica had the second-best sales record, and Paul was complaining to her about the number of late shipments to his customers and asked if she had the same problem. She responded, "I can't remember when I have had a late shipment, Paul. The support staff and Victor's team do a great job of getting my orders filled on time."

When Paul went to the sales manager, Carroll, to complain about the problem, he learned a few things. Carroll told him about being in the warehouse earlier when Paul was ranting at Victor. He also told Paul that as soon as he stormed away, Victor and his team started laughing and one of the stock boys mimicked Paul's tirade while the others applauded.

Carroll told Paul that his accusatory approach to the problem was only reinforcing the situation because the others were having so much fun at his expense. Carroll offered a suggestion about how to handle it differently. "Paul, the only time you ever say anything to the support people here is when something has gone wrong. They resent that and they have learned that they can get under your skin by delaying one of your orders now and then. I asked Victor what was going on and he said they just did it to have a little fun with you and they made sure that they picked a different customer each time so they would not have much impact on customer satisfaction."

Paul reacted, "I hope you told them to stop." Carroll responded, "Yes, I did, Paul, but you need to help. I suggest that you make it a point to visit the warehouse when you are here just to say thanks for helping to serve your customers. It would be a good idea to do that for the administrative staff too. I have heard a few of them talking about how you ignore them and they are part of the team too."

CONTINUED

"I don't have time to go around thanking everybody for doing their jobs," Paul said. Carroll replied, "Paul, they deserve to know that what they do makes a difference. Watch Veronica when she visits the office. She always stops to chat with the administrative staff and the warehouse team. She even sent a big thank-you card to everyone here a couple of weeks ago when they got a special rush order out to a big customer for her. The card is still on the bulletin board and everyone was exchanging high fives when they put it up there."

What message did Paul send to the headquarters personnel when he did not acknowledge their efforts?

_____

_____

What message did Veronica send to the same people by chatting with them and sending a thank-you card?

_____

_____

Is it any surprise that the headquarters people were more inclined to get all of Veronica's orders filled on time even though Paul accounted for more sales? People thrive on attention and if they don't get positive attention, they will settle for negative attention rather than be ignored. The warehouse group found a way to get a little attention from Paul.

Was Carroll, the sales manager, critical of Paul?   ❑ Yes   ❑ No

If you answered *yes*, read again what Carroll said to Paul. There are no disapproving words and Paul was not told that what he had been doing was wrong. He was encouraged to change his behavior and was told what might produce better results. Carroll did not compare Paul's behavior with Veronica's. Telling Paul how Veronica managed her relationships with the headquarters team gave him an example of how to let people know that they are appreciated.

Putting "Money in the Bank"

Knowing that people always need at least some attention and that they are more likely to make an extra effort for those who give them positive attention, it is worthwhile to start looking for opportunities to give a little more attention to everyone with whom you interact. It is like putting money in the bank. That small investment of time and energy will pay dividends of greater loyalty and higher productivity.

It also makes it easier to have successful interactions with others when things are not going so smoothly. When you are a source of positive attention for others, it is easier for them to hear and accept negative feedback without becoming defensive.

One of the challenges for many people in implementing this strategy is the tendency to think of positive attention as giving compliments or praise. Those are indeed examples of positive attention, but too many compliments or words of praise can begin to sound insincere, and it takes a lot of work to keep finding new things to compliment. Because of this, people tend to stop giving praise or compliments after a short while.

Ways to Give Positive Attention

To make sure that you continue to be a source of positive attention for others, identify more ways to do it. List below as many forms of appropriate, respectful attention as you can.

_____   _____
_____   _____
_____   _____
_____   _____
_____   _____
_____   _____
_____   _____
_____   _____
_____   _____
_____   _____

Were you able to think of 20 ways to give some kind of attention to others?

Compare your responses with the authors' suggestions in the Appendix.

The Value of Feedback on the Job

Sometimes managers express concern about having to give feedback frequently to employees. They wonder if people will start expecting it all of the time and whether they will have time to do it all of the time. Some object to having to do it because "they should do their jobs because that's what they are paid to do."

But even a small amount of positive attention will work wonders with your employees. You will not have to devote a great amount of time to giving feedback for it to make an important difference in the morale and productivity of your team.

Research has demonstrated that money is not the powerful motivator that many managers think it is. People often leave for lower-paying jobs when they believe they will get other needs satisfied in the new job. Being appreciated and having opportunities to grow or to have a better life balance are often more important to people than how much they are paid.

People need frequent feedback to develop into top performers. Without feedback, employees have no way to know if they are meeting your expectations and doing their jobs satisfactorily. Whether your direct reports are hourly workers or executives, they need and deserve frequent feedback if they are to do their best.

Guidelines for Delivering Feedback

When you give feedback to people about their performance, follow these guidelines to help them learn, improve, and grow.

➤ **Focus your feedback on behavior**

The idea is to help the person understand what they are doing well or what they could do better. You are not judging their worth as a person. You are not saying anything about their character.

➤ **Describe the behavior factually and specifically**

You are not judging the person or questioning their motivation. It is okay to communicate approval (such as, you did a good job), but all the person learns is that somehow they managed to please you. This gives no idea what specific behavior won your approval. When giving feedback about a behavior that you want to be changed, it is important to avoid negative judgment. That will only invite defensiveness and decrease the probability of behavior change.

➤ **Explore ideas and alternatives**

Good coaches know that people learn more when they think and figure things out for themselves as opposed to having someone just tell them what to do. Give employees an opportunity to share ideas about how to improve or how to resolve a problem and they will learn to do more of their own thinking. It is a subtle way to empower people and help them develop confidence in their own abilities.

➤ **Choose a time and place for giving personal feedback**

Many supervisors and managers naturally tend to ask employees to come to their offices for feedback discussions. Do you remember when you first learned about being called to the office? Is your employee going to be comfortable, receptive, and ready to learn when they arrive in your office? Some managers give feedback to employees in the presence of other employees. This can be embarrassing for the employee when it is negative feedback, and some people prefer to receive positive feedback privately.

The ideal location for giving feedback is where the recipient is most likely to feel comfortable. If the employee has an office, have your feedback discussion in his or her office. If that is not a possibility, meet in a conference room, have lunch together where you can talk comfortably and privately, or take a walk together. If you choose to meet in your office, be sure to shut off telephone calls and prevent other interruptions. This demonstrates respect for the other person and also communicates to him or her that your discussion is important.

Timing is also important for helping the recipient hear and learn from the feedback. Choose a time when the employee is least likely to be under a lot of stress. Avoid end-of-cycle deadlines or your usually busy periods, for example. It is not a good idea to stop someone in a hallway and start giving feedback, so make an appointment. Remember too, that the sooner you provide feedback the more likely your feedback will have the desired impact on behavior (reinforcing desirable behavior or changing undesirable behavior).

IS THIS GOOD FEEDBACK?

Read the feedback examples below and evaluate them using the criteria just explained. Check (√) the box for your evaluation. If the example does not deserve a good rating, explain why on the line provided.

1. "Your presentation in the meeting today was pretty dry and boring. Maybe a little humor would help."

   ❏ Good   ❏ Fair   ❏ Poor

   _____

2. "You finished the project ahead of schedule and under budget. Excellent work."

   ❏ Good   ❏ Fair   ❏ Poor

   _____

3. "Pat, I am concerned about the number of times you have arrived after starting time. Today was the third time during the past two weeks."

   ❏ Good   ❏ Fair   ❏ Poor

   _____

4. "Alex, several people have complained to me about your attitude lately. You probably need to work on that."

   ❏ Good   ❏ Fair   ❏ Poor

   _____

5. "Well, your work has been above average so I am going to give you a good rating this time."

   ❏ Good   ❏ Fair   ❏ Poor

   _____

CONTINUED

6. "Courtney, your sales improved 12% over this same period last year and three of your customers sent us e-mail messages with positive comments about your extra efforts to provide good service. I'm impressed."

❑ Good   ❑ Fair   ❑ Poor

_____

Now think of some feedback you recently gave to an employee that did not fit the criteria for "good" feedback and write it on the lines provided. On the lines below that, write why you think it did not fit the criteria.

Feedback given:

_____

_____

Why it was not "good":

_____

_____

Compare your answers with those of the authors in the Appendix.

WHAT WOULD YOU SAY?

Being able to recognize when feedback is done well and when it is not is an important first step. The next step is to practice giving feedback skillfully. On the lines below each of the following examples, write what you would say to give feedback skillfully.

1. Maria has prepared a PowerPoint presentation for you. She completed it two days before the deadline, used some creative graphics, and made no errors.

   _____

   _____

   _____

2. Sayeed facilitated the planning session for the important new project your team has been assigned. You noticed that he often interrupted others when they offered suggestions and told them that the session was restricted to defining and clarifying the objectives and that tactics would be discussed in the next meeting. Several members of the team seemed to withdraw and said little during the last half of the meeting.

   _____

   _____

   _____

3. Phillipe, your newest employee, completed his first assignment and the work was acceptable. The time required was longer than you expected and you are wondering why.

   _____

   _____

   _____

CONTINUED

4. Kathleen seems to be struggling with several of the people she supervises. You have observed her correcting their errors in front of others and speaking rather angrily when they seemed to have difficulty understanding her instructions.

_____

_____

_____

Now take another look at the previous exercise and the feedback you gave one of your employees. Write what would qualify as "good" feedback. From the previous exercise rewrite your feedback to make it fit the "good" criteria.

_____

_____

_____

Compare your feedback with the authors' suggested responses in the Appendix.

Exercise Review

In the first situation you have an opportunity to reinforce desirable behavior. Many managers would just say "Thank you" or "Nice job, Maria." Gratitude and praise are always appreciated and probably will have the desired reinforcement effect, but specific feedback would be more appreciated and would be even more likely to reinforce the behavior described.

In situation #2, you are faced with a less than satisfactory performance and an opportunity to help an employee improve. Sayeed will benefit from specific feedback about what he did and a discussion of what he could do differently to keep people involved and committed to the process and the results.

In situation #3, the new employee has done a good job and deserves positive feedback about the quality of his work. Perhaps you would not be concerned about a new employee taking more time with his first assignment. What are some reasons that a new person might take longer?

_____

_____

_____

Phillipe may have been very careful and meticulous with his first assignment to make sure it was done well. He may have taken longer because he has not yet learned where supplies can be found or who can provide the information he needs. He may have had to correct mistakes caused by anxiety that he will be less likely to feel after he is more familiar with the work and the organization.

It is okay for you to give feedback about the time, to engage Phillipe in a discussion of any problems he encountered, and to ask him how you might help. This would be a good time to ask him what ideas he has about how he will do the work next time.

In the fourth situation, your employee seems to need help. If Kathleen continues to handle people the way you have observed, she will likely have even more difficulty while her performance and the performance of her team suffers. She needs specific feedback about her behavior and options for handling the mistakes more skillfully. Remember to ask for her ideas about how to improve the process. She may need for you to teach her how to give feedback and to do some role-play practice to help develop her skills.

CASE STUDY: Kelly's Coaching Approach

Anna, an engineer and computer expert who is very organized and productive, had a history of being abrupt with people when they made mistakes or had difficulty understanding explanations or instructions. Her manager, Kelly, had given Anna some feedback about this behavior in the past but was aware that she still did it, particularly when nearing project deadlines.

Kelly decided to take a different approach, hoping to get Anna to work more effectively with others. While having lunch with Anna, she asked, "Are you aware that when we start getting close to deadlines that you fall back into that behavior of being impatient and somewhat abrupt with others?"

Anna acknowledged that she was aware that she did and said, "I guess when I am under stress I have a hard time being patient." Kelly replied, "I can understand that, Anna. We all are challenged to be appropriate with others when we are stressed ourselves. What do you think you can do about handling your stress more effectively so you won't offend others?"

Anna thought for a few moments and answered, "One thing that helps me deal with stress is some physical activity. When I have a lot of work to get done and time is running short, I tend to work through lunch, grab a sandwich from the vending machine, and skip my walk. Maybe it would be a good idea to take my walk or jog up and down the stairs a while instead of staying at my desk."

Kelly said, "Some physical activity might help you relax a little, relieve some tension. Good idea, Anna. Will you do that?" Anna replied, "Yes. I will. I don't want people to be upset with me. I need their support."

What was different about the manager's approach in this situation?

_____

_____

Many managers would have been tempted to remind Anna that her behavior they had discussed earlier was still occurring and to insist that it stop. This could easily lead to her becoming defensive or making empty promises in response to feeling pressured or criticized. Kelly used the coaching approach of asking questions. Her initial question was to determine if Anna knew that she still was abrupt at certain times. The question contained a description of the behavior and also invited Anna to acknowledge her awareness of doing it.

The second question invited Anna to think of a solution. People often are aware that they need to make a change and they have the ability to figure out how to do it. Sometimes they just need someone to serve as a catalyst and asking some questions in a caring manner can be all they need to think of what they need to do.

Improving Your Effectiveness Through Rapport

Choosing the words and following the feedback guidelines for what you say are very important. Without skillfully selected words, your feedback communication is unlikely to be successful.

As important as the words are, though, they are not the only component of effective feedback. As a coach, you will also want to establish *rapport* with your employees or whomever you are coaching.

Rapport is difficult to define because it is such an intangible thing that occurs between people. The dictionary defines it as "a harmonious accord." How would you define rapport?

_____

_____

Most people think of rapport as "clicking with someone" or "getting on the same frequency" with another person. It is a difficult thing to define because it is an intangible phenomenon that occurs between people. When we have rapport with another person we feel it. Both of us feel comfortable and connected.

Most of us go through life being dependent on rapport happening accidentally. We have rapport with some people; we don't have rapport with others. But you can help create rapport with most people you encounter rather than waiting and hoping for it to occur.

Pacing to Create Rapport

Researchers have noticed that when people have rapport, they mirror each other in many ways. They speak at about the same speed, the same volume, the same intensity. They even sit or stand in similar positions, move at about the same moment, reach for their beverages almost simultaneously, and so on. This mirroring or matching has come to be known as *pacing*.

To *pace* someone consciously requires paying attention to things you may not typically notice:

> ➤ **Speed (pace)**—fast, medium, or slow rate of talking, getting down to business, making decisions

> ➤ **Voice**—loud, soft, intense, relaxed, soothing, commanding

> ➤ **Facial expression**—happy, stressed, anxious, frustrated, angry, animated, poker face

> ➤ **Mood/emotion**—excited, disappointed, frustrated, angry, concerned

> ➤ **Appearance**—formal, casual, intense, relaxed, orderly, precise, comfortable

> ➤ **Posture/movements**—upright, tense, relaxed, animated, gestures, little movement

By adjusting your pace to that of the other person, you help him to be comfortable with you. The idea is to match the other person's mood. Mirror his posture (the same, but reversed like looking in a mirror). If the other person uses his hands a lot while talking, you use your hands in similar ways when you talk. But you do not have to match everything and you do not have to be exactly alike to achieve rapport.

With some emotions such as anxiety or anger, do not match the emotion. In such cases, people will feel more connected if you use words and body language to communicate a complementary emotion such as comforting or concern. People need to "feel" that you care.

At first, you likely will feel self-conscious and a little awkward while doing this, but the important thing is that the other person will feel more connected and won't even know why. Like any technique, this can be overdone or can be done poorly. Common sense tells you not to mirror inappropriate gestures. But with a little practice you will be able do it comfortably and skillfully enough to help create rapport with most people.

Matching Personality Style

Probably the most powerful form of pacing that will help to create a strong rapport with others is to recognize and match their personality type of style. Once you have identified the other person's style, then you can communicate in that style enough to create and maintain rapport.

This is important when giving feedback to help people feel comfortable and understand what you are communicating. They will be most receptive and learn more from the feedback when you give it in the style that is most natural for them.

Four Personality Styles

There are many ways to describe personality styles. The four-category approach presented here is easy to remember. Everyone possesses traits from all four styles, yet one style will be dominant. With practice, you can use this approach to assess others quickly and accurately.

Directing/Guiding

People who have this style as their dominant one are intense, fast-paced, results-oriented people who are direct and forceful in their communications. They have strongly held beliefs and opinions and tend to talk about them frequently. They also are proud of their accomplishments and will talk about them with others. Beyond those topics, they tend to be private and are uncomfortable with closeness and more personal topics.

Key characteristics to use for identification:

> ➤ Faster pace

> ➤ Impersonal style

> ➤ Actions, results are important

> ➤ Direct and authoritative

> ➤ Body language that says "ready for action", intense, rigid

Analytical

Those who are primarily *analytical* are slower-paced, perfectionistic, careful people who plan, schedule, research, and then act. They also are not comfortable with self-disclosure and prefer to keep things impersonal by focusing on facts, figures, concepts, problems, solutions, and the like. This is the most intellectual group and they may use words that most other people do not know. They sometimes seem detached or aloof and rarely display emotion.

Key characteristics to use for identification:

➤ Slower pace

➤ Impersonal style

➤ Information, facts, figures, details, scheduling are important

➤ Formal and reserved

➤ Measured, careful body language that says "think before you act"

Supporting/Caring

People who have this personality style are slower-paced, warm, personal, and friendly. They value relationships above all else, which makes them natural team players who enjoy working with others. They are self-disclosing and talk comfortably about all kinds of personal things but are primarily interested in others. They are the caretakers and peacekeepers who are always doing nice things for others. This group may tell you what you want to hear rather than what they really think or feel to make sure they do not offend or cause conflict.

Key characteristics to use for identification:

➤ Slower pace

➤ Personal style

➤ Empathetic, warm, nurturing, and sensitive

➤ Less assertive, smiley, and soft-spoken

➤ Body language that says "comforting and approachable"

Expressive

People who are mostly *expressive* are fast-paced, energetic, lively, animated people who are spontaneous, creative, and emotional. They react to almost all situations emotionally and spontaneously and seem to be in constant motion. Their facial expressions change frequently and reveal whatever is going on inside. They thrive on attention and are very good at getting attention. They often are flamboyant, loud, funny, and exaggerated. They can be charming and witty or rebellious depending on rapidly changing moods and the behavior of others around them.

Key characteristics to use for identification:

> ➤ Faster pace

> ➤ Personal style

> ➤ Dramatic, energetic, playful, and emotional

> ➤ Very reactive; tend to say what they feel

> ➤ Body language that says "look at me"

MATCHING FEEDBACK TO PERSONALITY

Using the letters below, identify which personality type/style would most appreciate the following types of feedback or attention.

D = Directing/Guiding   A = Analytical   S = Supporting/Caring   E = Expressive

_____ 1. Ask about them and their family.

_____ 2. Give them a plaque or trophy.

_____ 3. Give them tickets to a game or concert.

_____ 4. Thank them for offering to help.

_____ 5. Compliment them for being thorough and accurate.

_____ 6. Get excited about their project being done.

_____ 7. Ask for an appointment to discuss their project.

_____ 8. Tell them what you want done and when the work is due.

_____ 9. Give them a plant for their office.

_____ 10. Ask for their opinion about how to improve results.

Compare your answers with those of the authors in the Appendix.

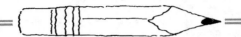

GIVING FEEDBACK IN DIFFERENT STYLES

Practice tailoring your feedback to the style of the recipient. Read the two situations below and then on the lines provided, write different feedback for each personality style.

Situation 1

The employee has completed a complex project (you can decide what it was) and the work was quite good. Give positive feedback matching the style of the employee.

Directing/Guiding style:

_____

_____

_____

Analytical style:

_____

_____

_____

Supporting/Caring style:

_____

_____

_____

Expressive style:

_____

_____

_____

CONTINUED

Situation 2

The employee's productivity has dropped in recent weeks. You have not noticed anything that would explain the change in performance. Give feedback about what you have observed [choose the type of work you want to address] as a step toward engaging the person in a conversation that might reveal the cause of the reduced productivity. Your objective is to get the productivity back to the desired level.

Directing/Guiding style:

_____

_____

_____

Analytical style:

_____

_____

_____

Supporting/Caring style:

_____

_____

_____

Expressive style:

_____

_____

_____

Compare your work with the authors' responses in the Appendix.

Guiding Others to

Be Their Best

The purpose of setting goals should be to increase opportunities for positive reinforcement."

–Aubrey C. Daniels, *Bringing Out the Best in People*

Setting Goals for What to Teach

Coaching sometimes requires you to help someone learn something new or to develop a new skill. Before you set out to teach someone, it is important to have well-defined goals.

A goal is a statement of a planned outcome. It is not a plan or a list of action steps. A goal is a statement of the result you intend to achieve when the plan has been executed and the action steps have been completed.

When training someone, it is helpful to state the goal as a *learning objective*. The emphasis is on what you want the other person to learn. In coaching, this learning objective is likely to be how to do something. Usually the goal will be stated in terms of behavior.

Performance requires more than understanding or acquiring information. It also requires knowing how to use that information to make decisions, choose courses of action, and do certain things to produce the desired result. Developing skill in any task or job takes practice.

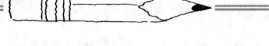

WHAT IS A GOOD LEARNING OBJECTIVE?

Evaluate the learning objectives below. Rate each one and place a check (√) to indicate if it is good, fair, or poor. For any you rate fair or poor, explain why in the space provided.

1. Employee will know how to handle an irate customer.
   ❑ Good   ❑ Fair   ❑ Poor
   _____

2. Employee will be able to use Microsoft Excel to create spreadsheets for our projects.
   ❑ Good   ❑ Fair   ❑ Poor
   _____

3. Employee will use empathetic listening and pacing skills to defuse anger.
   ❑ Good   ❑ Fair   ❑ Poor
   _____

4. Employee will set up and operate the machine without error.
   ❑ Good   ❑ Fair   ❑ Poor
   _____

5. Employee will prepare and deliver presentations.
   ❑ Good   ❑ Fair   ❑ Poor
   _____

6. Employee will learn about the three new products.
   ❑ Good   ❑ Fair   ❑ Poor
   _____

Now practice writing a learning objective for something you might teach.

_____
_____
_____

Compare your answers with those of the authors in the Appendix.

Following a Training Methodology

When you have a well-defined learning objective, the next step is to plan how [you] will teach the person. The approach you use may be determined partially by the situation. For example, if the person is in a different location from you, you may [not] be able to provide one-on-one instruction.

Most people think of the teaching part of coaching as telling and showing someone how to do something. It is also important for the learner to actually do it.

Four Steps to Effective Training

The following tried-and-true training formula works well for most learning situations:

1. Tell them how to do it

2. Show them how to do it

3. Have them tell and show you how to do it

4. Have them do it

In his book *Coaching for Performance*[*], John Whitmore reports on research that originally was done by IBM and later was replicated by the United Kingdom Postal Service. A group was divided randomly into three subgroups and each subgroup was taught the identical simple procedure. A different approach was used with each group. The table below shows the amount of learning that each group was able to recall after the training was completed.

	Told	Told & Shown	Told, Shown, Experienced
Recall after 3 weeks	70%	72%	85%
Recall after 3 months	10%	32%	65%

[*]John Whitmore, *Coaching for Performance*, p. 22

As effective as the tell-show-do formula has been, it can be made to work even better when you apply pacing during the instruction. By matching the learner's pace and personality style, you make it easier for that person to learn from you. If you teach in your natural style but it is different from the learner's style, that person will be less likely to learn quickly and effectively from you.

tanding Perception Systems

...crease the effectiveness of your coaching by tailoring the instruction to
...ier's learning style. And a significant factor in learning style is a person's
...inant *perception system*.

Three Categories

All people are equipped with five sensory systems: seeing, hearing, tasting,
smelling, and touching/feeling. Even if one or more of these systems is damaged
or inoperative because of birth, disease, or accident, everyone has the "hardware"
and "software" for all five senses.

Human beings use the senses of smell and taste less than do some other life forms,
so we categorize people into just three groups. Each of us is a blend of all five
sensory systems with one that is strongest or most dominant.

Those who depend primarily on the sense of sight are known as *visual* people.
Those who depend most on hearing are *auditory*, and those who depend primarily
on the sense of touch are *kinesthetic*.

With people you know well, it may be easy for you to figure out which sensory
system they use the most. The person who sends you many e-mail messages may
be a visual. The person who almost always uses the telephone to communicate
with you is likely an auditory. The person who usually drops in or catches you in
the hallway and talks while walking is probably a kinesthetic.

Recognizing the Dominant System

To assess which style is dominant, pay attention to how a person does things,
how he prefers to communicate, how he makes decisions, how he participates in
meetings, and so on. And pay attention to the individual's vocabulary. Each of us
has developed a vocabulary with more words that are related to our dominant
system. These words are known as "referents"—they refer to the dominant sense.

Below are examples of words and phrases that refer to the different learning styles.

VISUAL	AUDITORY	KINESTHETIC
Get the picture?	Hear what I'm saying?	Do you grasp the concept?
Show me how this works.	Sounds good to me.	How does that fit for you?
See what I mean?	Tell me about your trip.	Run down the itinerary for me.
Look this over for me.	Does that ring any bells?	
That was illuminating.	I really enjoyed chatting with you.	Let's make it happen.
I have just a glimmer of an idea.	I need to talk it over with Ann.	Something doesn't feel right here.
Very good insight.	They really sang your praises.	Can't quite put my finger on it.
		I sense some reluctance.

When listening to what people say or reading what they write, notice the frequency and consistency of word choices in each style until you have detected a definite dominance. Much like solving a mystery, a single clue is not sufficient. It is the consistent and repeated use of referents that will *reveal* (visual) the dominance, *tell* (auditory) you which style is dominant, or *tip* (kinesthetic) you off.

Relating Perception System to Learning Style

It is most important to recognize the perception system when a person has a strong dominance in one style because they will learn most effectively through that style. Fortunately, such individuals are easy to recognize. Some people have only a slight dominance in one system and will be able to learn well in two learning styles. Let's look at how perception system relates to learning style.

Visual Learning

Visual people need to *see* it to get it. They trust what they can see more than what they hear or feel. They remember best what they *saw* and may not remember what they heard or did or how they felt. It is as though they have a video recorder in their brains able to recall those images with great accuracy.

Visual learners will learn best when you can show them what you want them to learn. Use written materials, visual aids, pictures, charts, and graphs. If you are teaching them about a product or how to use a tool or machine, have the product or tool there for them to see while you explain. Demonstrate step by step as you tell them what to do. Remember, they need to see what you are talking about. Remember, too, to use visual words.

Visuals think with mental pictures, forming images in their minds. They can visualize in great detail. About 40–45% of adults are primarily visual learners.

Auditory Learning

Auditory people need to *hear* it. They like to discuss things, ask lots of questions, and listen carefully to the answers. They listen well and remember what they *heard* better than what they saw or did or how they felt. Auditory people enjoy listening to books on tape or CD, and talk radio or TV shows featuring interviews and discussion. They remember conversations and song lyrics with accuracy.

Auditory learners learn best when you talk them through what you want them to learn. As you explain something, be prepared to answer questions. They learn by listening and asking. Ask them to tell you what they have heard you say. Telling you what they understand helps them learn and remember. You can demonstrate and provide written materials but be sure to verbalize everything and do not expect them to learn by just watching or reading. Be sure to use auditory vocabulary as you explain and answer their questions.

Auditory people often do not read a great deal, and they may not remember much of what they read. When they read, they need to hear the words and may sub-vocalize while they read or even say the words aloud. They think with mental dialogue and carry on an internal conversation while they think through something. Only about 10% of adults are auditory learners.

Kinesthetic Learning

Kinesthetic people have to *do* it to get it. They like to touch, feel, do, and be involved. They are good with their hands. They need to move their bodies and experience things. They remember best what they *did* and how they felt when doing it.

Kinesthetic learners are the true "hands on" learners who need to touch something, use it, manipulate it, disassemble and reassemble it to understand how it works. Plan to have them physically doing things early. While you demonstrate and explain, have them do each step with you. Emotional involvement is also important for this group so make the training lively and fun. Emphasize the actions, results to be achieved, and the payoffs for learning to do it well. Their frame of reference is all about doing and feeling. They will understand and remember more if you use action words and emotional words.

Kinesthetic people trust their intuition and emotions for decision making and may not be able to explain how they knew what to do. "It just felt right." About 40–45% of adults are kinesthetic learners.

Practice identifying the dominant style of the people in the case study that follows.

CASE STUDY: A Team Meeting

You enter the meeting room and notice that several people are already in the room. Courtney is sitting at the conference table reading a report. Kevin is listening carefully as Beth talks enthusiastically about what she did over the weekend. Donovan is sitting at the far end of the table swinging back and forth in the swivel chair and twirling his pencil like a baton.

When the meeting begins, Kevin asks if it will be okay for him to use his laptop computer to take notes during the meeting. Courtney asks Kevin if he will send her a copy of his notes because she needs to use her computer for the presentation she will be giving during the meeting. He agrees to do that for her and asks you, Beth, and Donovan if he should send you the notes too. Beth replies, "No, thank you. I never review the notes anyway." Donovan says, "Sure, shoot 'em over to me too."

You ask Courtney to start the meeting with her presentation. She turns on the projector and starts her presentation by saying, "I will be showing you the status of our new product development and you will see that we are ahead of schedule and it looks like we will be able to finish the project early. This first slide also illustrates how we have managed to save quite a bit of money by incorporating designs from the earlier prototypes."

Beth asks, "Are you saying that we not only are ahead of schedule but we also are under budget?" Courtney confirmed that this was accurate and Beth replies, "I'm glad to hear that." Donovan smacks his hand on the table and says, "Way to go, Courtney."

Kevin speaks up and says, "Courtney, I see on your graph that you are projecting a completion date almost three weeks earlier than we planned. Will you be showing us how this will affect the marketing strategy and product introduction?" Courtney replies, "Yes, Kevin. Look at this matrix on the next slide and you will see that what I envision is using the extra time to arrange more focus groups and test markets before the full rollout to help ensure that we eliminate all of the bugs." Kevin says, "This looks really good, Courtney."

What is the dominant learning/communication style of each of the team members?

Courtney: _____

Beth: _____

Kevin: _____

Donovan: _____

Compare your answers with the authors' responses in the Appendix.

CATERING TO DIFFERENT LEARNING STYLES

Select a learning objective that is relevant to what you do in your organization and plan how you will coach employees on what you want them to learn.

Visual Learner

Name: _____   Objective: _____

1. How will you structure the training to help this person learn most effectively?

   _____

   _____

   _____

2. What will you say to teach the person what you want him to understand or be able to do?

   _____

   _____

   _____

   _____

   _____

   _____

Auditory Learner

Name: _____   Objective: _____

1. How will you structure the training to help this person learn most effectively?

   _____

   _____

   _____

2. What will you say to teach the person what you want her to understand or be able to do?

   _____

   _____

   _____

   _____

   _____

   _____

CONTINUED

Kinesthetic Learner

Name: _____ Objective: _____

1. How will you structure the training to help this person learn most effectively?

   _____

   _____

   _____

2. What will you say to teach the person what you want her to understand or be able to do?

   _____

   _____

   _____

   _____

   _____

Share with others the information about the different learning styles and ask them to give you feedback about your practice exercise above. Having someone else evaluate your work and discuss it with you will help you think of more ideas about how to tailor your training.

It is natural for each of us to teach someone else using our own dominant style of learning and communicating. This works fine when the learner has the same dominant style. Learners with a different dominant style, however, will be less likely to learn as rapidly or as effectively, and you will likely be frustrated and disappointed with their performance. It is important for you to recognize and match their dominant style in all of your coaching efforts.

Also remember that feedback is an important part of the learning process. Giving feedback skillfully while people are learning can help them learn.

Coaching Others to Learn from Their Mistakes

Mistakes are a learning opportunity. As a coach, you can help people learn from their mistakes.

Take a look at your organization. What happens to people when they make a mistake? The following are common outcomes. Check (√) all that are true in your organization.

- ❑ Reprimanded by supervisor
- ❑ Fired or suspended
- ❑ Ridiculed or teased by co-workers
- ❑ Required to pay for the cost
- ❑ Report is placed in their personnel file
- ❑ No longer trusted by supervisor
- ❑ The mistake is ignored and no one says anything

All but the last one are harsh responses for making a mistake. Everyone makes mistakes and when a mistake results in this kind of treatment, some predictable lessons are learned, such as the following:

1. **Quality is not important.** If the mistake is ignored and nothing is said, the lesson is that mistakes are not a problem so there is no need to be concerned about quality or accuracy.

2. **Perfection is required.** Harsh responses teach that you do not want to make mistakes in this organization. Employees figure out quickly that regardless of what the job description or performance agreement says, the true expectation is no mistakes. When they realize that is the expectation, they will become anxious about making mistakes, will become reluctant to take risks, and will resist change to continue doing things the way they already know to avoid making mistakes. Innovation and creativity are dead.

3. **Hide your mistakes.** When mistakes result in punishment or harsh treatment, employees learn to do whatever is necessary to keep mistakes from being discovered. Accountability is replaced with deniability.

It is costly for any organization when employees fear mistakes and approach their work with anxiety and extreme caution and attempt to hide mistakes or deny responsibility. You can coach employees to stop fearing mistakes and become more trusting and comfortable with accountability.

A Five-Step Approach

Here is a five-step coaching approach for helping people learn from a mistake. It is important to use all five steps. It also is important to complete each step before moving to the next one.

Step 1: Demonstrate Respect

Say or do nothing to communicate disapproval, disgust, disappointment, anger, or other negative feelings. The person is already feeling bad. He may be fearing some punishment or ridicule because of how past mistakes were handled by parents, teachers, siblings, or supervisors and he is expecting the same from you. He also is likely to be judging himself and saying disapproving things in his internal dialogue. If you sigh in frustration, roll your eyes, or say, "Why did you…?"—he will only feel worse, which reduces the probability of his learning anything productive from the mistake.

You may want to do more than be respectful; you may want to show the person that you care by being supportive and reassuring. Say, "That's okay. We all make mistakes." Or "Don't beat up on yourself. You just made a mistake."

Even if it is a big mistake or a costly mistake, it is important for you to communicate with sincerity that it was a mistake, which can happen to anyone. This will help prepare the person for learning from the experience rather than learning the other lessons mentioned above.

Step 2: Share One of Your Own Mistakes

To demonstrate that you are sincere when you reassure people and tell them that we all make mistakes, tell them about one of your own mistakes. If you have made the same kind of mistake, tell them briefly about when and where you did it and how you felt. You can tell them about an even bigger mistake you made and what that was like. Keep it brief because you want to move on to helping the person learn from the mistake.

This step also helps people relax and feel better. This is important because it is hard to learn when emotions are high. Getting the emotional level down closer to normal helps people learn. This step also builds rapport and trust in your relationship and greatly reduces the probability that people will hide mistakes from you in the future.

Step 3: Ask Your First Question

For people to learn from their mistakes, they must first realize how the mistake occurred. Your first question is directed to identify the cause of the error. You can ask, "How did this happen?"

When you ask this question, wait patiently with an expectant look on your face until the person answers. Be patient. The person may need more than a few seconds to think, compose herself, and figure out how to explain how the mistake happened. If you start talking before she answers, you may add to her anxiety and confusion.

What do you do if the person responds, "I don't know—it just got all fouled up"?

Continue to be patient and reassuring. It is hard for people to think when they have a lot of feelings and this response is a clue that they are still rattled. Ask again in a slightly different form such as, "That's okay, Pat. It can happen to anyone. It is important when something like this happens that we figure out how it happened. What do you think caused this?"

The person may now be able to tell you what was done incorrectly. If she cannot, then take this approach: Ask the person to show, tell, or walk you through the process step by step so you can figure out together how the mistake occurred. Even if you have already decided what was done incorrectly, it is important that you give the person the opportunity to discover it for herself. If you just tell people or point it out, you invite them to feel stupid. But when you work together to identify the cause, people feel supported and will learn more by being involved.

Only after the cause of the mistake has been identified do you proceed to step 4.

Step 4: Ask Your Second Question

The next question to ask is, "How can you fix it?" Not all mistakes can be fixed but you want to explore the options for fixing it if it is possible to do so.

Sometimes coaches may ask, "How can *we* fix it?" But it is better to use *you* than *we*, and here's why: Part of what you want people to learn when they have made a mistake is that even though it is okay and human to make a mistake now and then, it is important to be accountable and figure out how to repair the damage.

If the person cannot figure out a way to fix the problem and you know that it is possible to do some damage control, you become a teacher. You tell and show what to do and how to do it, have the person tell and show you, and have him do it with you there so you can give feedback and support. Then if the problem ever occurs again, he will know what to do even if you are not there.

Even when you think that it is not possible to undo the damage, you still want to ask the second question ("How can you fix it?"). The person may think of something that no one has ever considered before. Even if he cannot think of a way to fix the problem caused by his mistake, you still have demonstrated trust and confidence in his abilities, and that is a positive thing to do.

Step 5: Ask Your Final Question

You may have already realized what this last question will be: "How can you prevent it from happening again?"

Even though making a mistake is just being human and it is inevitable that all of us make mistakes now and then, it is not desirable to make the *same* mistake again. The purpose of using this coaching approach when people make mistakes is to help them learn to be accountable and to not repeat costly errors.

As before, when you ask this question, it is important for you to wait patiently and expectantly for the other person to provide the answer. Do not jump in and start teaching what to do without giving people the opportunity to figure it out on their own.

When people do their own thinking and find their own solutions, they get a much greater feeling of accomplishment and are much more likely to learn from the experience and remember what they learned. They have more of a feeling of ownership for the solution, which greatly increases the likelihood that they will remember the lesson and will not repeat the mistake.

When you use this coaching approach for responding to the mistakes made by others, they will learn to be more confident about approaching even challenging assignments. They also will learn to think more clearly when mistakes do occur and to take responsibility for finding solutions and preventive measures on their own. Rather than coming to you to fix it for them, they will become more independent and self-managing, which will free time for you to devote to other responsibilities. This is what empowerment is all about. Everybody wins.

Even though this approach seems to be simple and straightforward, it will require practice to learn to do it skillfully. Make a commitment to practice using this approach with your employees, your significant others, your children, and your co-workers. The more you do it, the better you will be able to apply it when serious mistakes occur.

You may have noticed that this approach to handling mistakes is another example of how coaching is often asking the right questions at the right time. The technique of asking questions that require responders to think and figure out things for themselves is a powerful way to help others learn.

Use the scenario on the next page to practice using the five-step model for coaching someone who has made a mistake.

CASE STUDY: Stacy Learns from Her Mistake

You were listening nearby as Stacy received a telephone call from a customer who was having difficulty with a software product. As Stacy listened carefully to the customer's description of the problem and asked several questions to understand what was not working properly, it was apparent that there was a communication problem with the customer.

After several minutes of attempting to clarify the difficulty with the customer, Stacy became agitated and began speaking with what sounded like controlled anger or disgust, "You will have to be more specific about what you have done or there is no way I can help you."

Apparently, the customer said something to Stacy in response that added to Stacy's frustration because her next statement to the customer was, "My supervisor won't be able to help you any better than I can because you are not making any sense."

After that statement, the customer terminated the call. You heard Stacy say while flinging the headset onto the desk, "Idiots should not even try to use computers."

Presumably this is not the way you want customers to be treated, and Stacy's handling of the situation is an important mistake. Fill in what you would say in each of the five steps below.

1. Demonstrate Respect/Support

_____

_____

_____

2. Share a Mistake

_____

_____

_____

3. Ask the First Question

_____

_____

_____

■ CONTINUED ■

Assume that Stacy does not immediately answer the question with a specific description of what was done incorrectly. How would you ask the first question differently to get an answer that indicates Stacy understands what was done poorly?

_____

4. Ask the Second Question

_____

Assume that Stacy suggests calling the customer with an apology, an offer to help with the problem, and a free upgrade for the latest version of the software. You agree that this would be a good idea.

5. Ask the Final Question

_____

Assume that Stacy suggests that, when feelings start rising with future calls, she use the stress-reduction technique of standing up and rotating her head, rolling her shoulders, bending her knees, taking a couple of deep breaths, and using an "I-statement" such as, "I am having difficulty understanding what is happening with the application. Will you please tell me step by step what you did so that I might pinpoint the problem?"

You agree that this should help prevent having the customer hang up with bad feelings toward your company and you offer to role-play the scenario with Stacy to provide immediate practice.

Helping people learn from their mistakes can be one of the most valuable coaching skills. Not only will people learn, they will value you and your skills and will grow in self-confidence and accountability.

Compare your responses with those of the authors in the Appendix.

A MISTAKE IN YOUR WORKPLACE

Think of a recent situation in your workplace in which an employee made a mistake. First describe that mistake on the lines provided and then plan how you will coach the employee on what you want him or her to learn from it.

The mistake:

_____

_____

_____

1. Demonstrate Respect/Support

_____

2. Share a Mistake

_____

3. Ask the First Question

_____

4. Ask the Second Question

_____

5. Ask the Final Question

_____

People often comment that they don't have time to coach people through mistakes when things go wrong because the situation demands immediate correction. There certainly will be times when you may need to take charge, make quick decisions and tell others what to do to respond to a situation. After the emergency, use the coaching approach and go through the five steps with the person to help them learn so the next time they will be able to act quickly on their own!

Using Listening Skills as a Coaching Tool

Listening is Good Business."

–Diana Bonet, *The Business of Listening*

Improving Listening Skills

In many interactions with others, the most important interpersonal skill is listening. No matter how skillfully one person chooses and delivers the words, communication does not occur if the other person does not listen. Good communicators know that good listening skills demonstrate respect for others and improve the odds for successful win-win interactions.

Effective coaches know that listening often can be more valuable than teaching. Often people have the experience, knowledge, and skills to accomplish what they need or want to do, but are not achieving for other reasons. They may not know what is blocking them, and a coach with skillful listening can help them identify the problem.

Ideally, a listener provides a response that proves to the speaker that he has been heard and understood. The ideal response also confirms for the listener that what was heard was understood accurately.

Most people go through their entire lives without receiving any instruction or training about how to listen. We all assume that because we have ears we know how to listen. But because we haven't been taught how to listen, most of us have learned by copying the listening behaviors of others, and we listen just the way everyone else does. Most of our own listening responses are predictable.

HOW WOULD YOU RESPOND?

On the lines provided, write your most likely response to each of the statements.

1. "These figures just don't make any sense and the explanations are horrible. Why don't they teach engineers how to communicate?"

_____

_____

2. "I heard that management is going to announce another layoff this week. If that's true, I bet I'm gone this time. Man, it sucks to be the newest person in the department."

_____

_____

3. "I have had it with Gunther. He has to be the most egotistical and incompetent person I have ever had to work with."

_____

_____

4. "Oh, no. I really messed up this spreadsheet and I have no idea what I did wrong. I just don't understand how this stuff works."

_____

_____

5. "Meetings, meetings, meetings. How are we supposed to get any work done when we spend half our time in meetings?"

_____

_____

6. "You really made me look bad in the meeting this morning. I thought you were my friend."

_____

_____

Identifying Common Listening Responses

The great majority of people respond to situations such as those in the preceding exercise in fairly predictable ways. What follows are some of the most commonly used listening responses with brief explanations and examples.

1. **Tell, Command**

   Telling the other person what to do. Directing them.

   Example: *"Calm down and think about your options."*

2. **Ask Questions**

   Asking fact-finding questions, seeking more details, or asking closed questions that can be answered *yes* or *no* or with a one-word response.

   Examples: *"What did he do to upset you?" "Did you check the manual?"*

3. **Offer Suggestions or Help**

   Trying to help the person by giving advice or suggestions or offering to help in some way.

   Examples: *"Maybe there is a class you could take." "I'm pretty good with that software. Want some help?"*

4. **Reassure, Encourage**

   Helping the person feel better by offering words of encouragement, reassurance. Being emotionally supportive.

   Examples: *"You'll be fine." "I know you can do it."*

5. **Preach, Moralize, Push Beliefs**

   Instead of telling what to do, you tell the person what they *should* do.

   Example: *"You should be careful about what you say. The boss likes Gunther."*

6. **Explain, Give Logical Reasons**

   Also known as lecturing, this response is an attempt to help someone understand.

   Example: *"Meetings are necessary because we need to communicate and combine efforts to be productive."*

7. Use Humor, Sidetrack, Withdraw

When we are uncomfortable with what the other person says, we often try to change the subject or withdraw from the situation or use humor to cope with our discomfort.

Examples: *"Man, you need to cut back on the coffee." "Oops. Gotta run. Hope it works out."*

8. Agree, Take Sides

This can be a form of commiserating or simply agreeing with the other person's statements.

Examples: *"You're not kidding. Those engineers might as well be speaking a foreign language."*

9. Apologize

When someone is upset with us, most of us will apologize (even if we did nothing wrong).

Example: *"I'm sorry. I didn't intend to make you look bad."*

10. Criticize, Disagree, Judge

Say something that is disapproving of the other person or argue with them.

Examples: *"You were wrong. I had to speak up." "You always blame others when you can't understand."*

RECOGNIZING THE RISKS OF SOME RESPONSES

Take a few minutes to go back to the previous exercise and reread your responses to the six example situations. Evaluate each response to learn if you used any of the common listening responses identified in the preceding section. Next to each of your responses, jot down the number of the common response you used (in some cases you may have used more than one).

In some situations, such responses carry risks. For each common response, think about how the other person might react and how that response might result in an unwanted reaction. Think about how it might cause a communication failure or might invite the other person to escalate or even damage a relationship.

Write on the lines provided how each type of response might have an unexpected, undesired outcome.

1. Tell, Command

Telling the other person what to do. Directing them.

_____

_____

2. Ask Questions

Asking fact-finding questions, seeking more details, or asking closed questions that can answered *yes* or *no* or with a one-word response.

_____

_____

3. Offer Suggestions or Help

Trying to help the person by giving advice or suggestions or offering to help in some way.

_____

_____

4. Reassure, Encourage

Helping the person feel better by offering words of encouragement, reassurance. Being emotionally supportive.

_____

_____

CONTINUED

CONTINUED

5. Preach, Moralize, Push Beliefs

Instead of telling what to do, you tell the person what they *should do*.

_____

_____

6. Explain, Give Logical Reasons

You provide information hoping to help them understand.

_____

_____

7. Humor, Sidetrack, Withdraw

When we are uncomfortable with what the other person says, we often try to change the subject or withdraw from the situation or use humor to cope with our discomfort.

_____

_____

8. Agree, Take Sides

This can be a form of commiserating or simply agreeing with the other person's statements.

_____

_____

9. Apologize

When someone is upset with us, most of us will apologize (even if we did nothing wrong).

_____

_____

10. Criticize, Disapprove, Judge

_____

_____

Compare your ideas with those of the authors in the Appendix.

The responses that most of us learned in childhood are not all wrong. But they do have some risks. Those risks are high when we are listening to someone in emotional turmoil or someone who may have a problem to be resolved. When people are relatively calm and having a normal conversation, the common responses are less risky and are less likely to cause any problems. A few of them can be problematical even in unemotional situations (1, 5, 10, for example). Most people do not like to be judged or criticized, and some people do not like for others to tell them what to do at any time.

How can you respond when you are listening to someone who has a problem or who is experiencing some powerful emotions? This will be addressed in the next section.

Being An Active Listener

Effective listeners get actively involved and make a conscious effort to understand what is being said. Most of us tend to be rather passive listeners—giving only partial attention to what others are saying while we think about what we want to say when we have an opportunity to speak.

Becoming a More Active Listener

Good coaching requires that you learn how to be a truly active listener. There are four ways to do this:

> **Attentive Silence**
>
> While remaining quiet, give subtle signals that you are paying attention to what the other person is saying by making good eye contact, nodding your head now and then, putting an interested expression on your face, and assuming an interested posture.

> **Attentive Words and Sounds**
>
> While doing all of the above, also make some sounds such as "Hmmm" or "Uh-huh" or say things such as "I see," "I hear you," "I understand."

> **Door Openers or Prompts**
>
> Encourage the other person to talk more by saying, "Please continue," "Go on," or "Tell me more," or by asking open-ended questions: "What else?" "Then what?" "What more do you want me to know?"

> **Restate or Paraphrase**
>
> Summarize what the other person said by restating at least some of the content and acknowledge the emotions the person seems to have. End your restatement with a check-out question at the end to signal that you are finished. "You've heard that there may be more layoffs and you're worried that you will lose your job. Right?"

All four of these techniques convey the message that you are interested and that you care about the other person and what he is saying. For that reason, people appreciate your using these techniques and will often want to talk more with you. Remember how much people crave attention?

Coaching Skills for Leaders

Evaluating Active Listening Responses

Do these active listening responses prove that you understand? Let's examine each one and answer that question.

Does *attentive silence* prove to the speaker that you have understood what she said?

    ❏ Yes   ❏ No

Do *attentive words and sounds* prove that you have understood what she said?

    ❏ Yes   ❏ No

Do *door openers* or *prompts* prove that you have understood what she said?

    ❏ Yes   ❏ No

If you checked *no* for each question, you are correct. The first three active listening techniques create only an impression of listening—they provide no real evidence that you have understood a word. They also do not provide you with any confirmation that what you have heard is an accurate understanding of what the other person intended to communicate to you. You may think you have understood, but if all you do is use one or all of the first three active listening responses, you cannot be sure that you are correct.

Does *restatement* or *paraphrasing* prove that you have understood what the person said?

    ❏ Yes   ❏ No   ❏ Maybe

The correct answer this time can be any one of the three. If you have listened carefully and you restate accurately, then the answer is *yes*. If you did not listen carefully and your restatement is incorrect, the answer is *no*.

But at least with paraphrasing and restatement, you have the opportunity for correction or clarification. This active listening skill can revolutionize your communication with people.

Three Cs of Good Communication

Anytime you use active listening technique #4—paraphrasing or restatement—you will receive one of these three responses: confirmation, correction, and clarification. Think of these as the *three Cs of good communication*. Let's take a look at each of these possible responses to paraphrasing.

> ➤ If you made a sincere attempt to listen carefully and restate accurately and your paraphrase was correct, how do you think the other person would respond?

_____

Typically, the speaker would *confirm* your accuracy and tell you more. People like being understood and will usually open up and talk more with someone who understands. This is an important benefit of using this technique. You prove to the other person that you understood what they said, and you receive confirmation that your understanding is correct.

> ➤ If you made a sincere attempt to listen carefully and restate accurately and your paraphrase was incorrect, how do you think the other person would respond?

_____

If you wrote that the other person would try to *correct* your misunderstanding, you are correct. People want to be understood, so if you misunderstand and restate incorrectly, they will tell you again what they said before in an effort to be understood. This is another benefit of using the technique. Isn't it better to learn immediately that your understanding was inaccurate than to proceed with the false assumption that you have communicated well?

> ➤ If you made a sincere attempt to listen carefully and restate accurately and your paraphrase was only partially correct, how do you think the other person would respond?

_____

If you are partially correct but missed an important point or just left out something that the other person wanted you to understand, he would *clarify* any shade of meaning that needed to be improved. This is another benefit of using the restatement technique.

You probably use active listening techniques #1 and #2 without even thinking, but you may have to practice using #3 and #4 to develop skill with them. All four are positive and have some value, but please remember that only the paraphrasing technique confirms understanding.

The Role of Empathy in Active Listening

What is your definition of empathy?

The most common answers for this question are "putting yourself in the other person's shoes," "getting in touch with the other person's feelings," or "sharing another's feelings." Dictionaries define *empathy* as "experiencing the feelings of another as one's own, or the capacity for this."

When people know you have empathy with them, they respond very positively. This is a powerful human experience. It is a powerful connection that leads to trust, openness, and sharing.

Empathy vs. Sympathy

The closest most people come to demonstrating empathy is to communicate *sympathy*, which is different from empathy. Sympathy is usually associated with distressing feelings, but it need not be. The defining feature is telling someone how *you* feel about what the person has told you. Someone tells you that she has just received a promotion and you say, "I'm happy for you." That is sympathy. You tell the person how *you* feel about their news. Someone tells you that his water pipes froze, flooded his basement, and damaged his photo albums, and you respond, "I'm sorry you lost your precious photos." Again, sympathy.

When you acknowledge how the *other person* is feeling, you demonstrate empathy—the ability to get in touch with their feelings. "You're really excited about this promotion, aren't you?" "You sound frustrated about the flooding and really sad about your photographs being damaged. Right?"

Feel the difference between sympathy and empathy? It is rare for someone to communicate empathy, and that is part of why it has such a powerful impact.

Demonstrating Empathy

Genuine empathy is greatly appreciated by others, so it is important to acknowledge feelings as part of the active listening paraphrasing technique. Restating content (information, ideas, opinions, concepts) proves understanding, and acknowledging the other person's emotions demonstrates empathy. Empathy and understanding are what active listening skill #4 is all about.

Step by step, the active listening feedback formula is:

1. Restate in paraphrase form the content of what the other person said—**Understanding**

2. Acknowledge the other person's feelings (either spoken or shown with body language)—**Empathy**

3. End with a check-out question to invite a response—**Confirmation**, **Correction**, or **Clarification**

Acknowledging the feelings of the other person is often the most difficult part. One reason is that we are often unaccustomed to talking about feelings. Many cultures teach to not verbalize feelings. Many people do not express feelings with words. Their feelings are communicated only through voice tones, volume, inflection, facial expressions, postures, and gestures. We all have learned to read those signals, but few of us have learned to talk about feelings.

Because we are not taught, developing this skill as an adult requires a lot of practice. After all, you are setting out to change a lifetime set of listening habits. The exercise on the next page will get you started.

ACKNOWLEDGE OTHERS' FEELINGS

In each of the examples below, the speaker does not communicate feelings with words. Imagine how this person sounds and how he looks as he says the words in the statements so that you can figure out how he might be feeling. Then on the lines provided, write a restatement or paraphrase so that it acknowledges the speaker's emotions. Include a check-out question at the end to invite the person to respond to your feedback. Read the first statement and restatement as an example.

Example Statement: "You really made me look bad in the meeting this morning. I thought you were my friend."

Restatement/Paraphrase: "You are angry about how I spoke about your presentation, aren't you?"

1. "These figures just don't make any sense and the explanations are horrible. Why don't they teach engineers how to communicate?"

   _____

   _____

2. "I heard that management is going to announce another layoff this week. If that's true, I bet I'm gone this time. Man, it stinks to be the newest person in the department."

   _____

   _____

3. "I have had it with Gunther. He has to be the most egotistical and incompetent person I have ever had to work with."

   _____

   _____

CONTINUED

4. "Oh, no. I really messed up this spreadsheet and I have no idea what I did wrong. I just don't understand how this stuff works."

_____

_____

5. "Meetings, meetings, meetings. How are we supposed to get any work done when we spend half our time in meetings?"

_____

_____

Compare your active listening responses with those
of the authors in the Appendix.

Dispelling Concerns About Paraphrasing

People just learning about the paraphrasing technique often express concerns about using it, and you may have some of these concerns too.

> **"Won't the other person think you are mimicking them?"**

If you are making a sincere effort to understand and have empathy, people usually will not notice that you are restating what they just said because they feel your sincerity and they receive evidence that you really did understand. When they hear their own feelings being acknowledged, they feel the empathy. It is rare for someone to react negatively when you are sincere. If you are not sincere in your effort but are only trying to manipulate them, they will sense that and respond defensively.

If you are using the technique with people who know you well, they may quickly sense that you are doing something that you have not done in the past and they may become somewhat defensive. If you explain briefly what you are doing and why you are doing it (to be sure you are understanding them accurately), they usually will see the potential value of this and will no longer be defensive. They may even respond, "Well, it's about time you learned how to listen."

> **"Don't other people get tired of your just restating all of the time?"**

As with any technique, active listening paraphrasing can be overdone. With continued practice you will become aware of how much is enough and how much is too much. The more emotional the other person is or the more important his problem is to him, the less likely he will even notice that you are restating time after time. What he will be aware of is how much you seem to care and how well you are understanding him.

> **"This sounds so mechanical to me. I wouldn't like someone doing that to me."**

When you first learn any new behavior, it will seem mechanical and even awkward or phony for a while. Have you ever operated an automobile with steering wheel and controls on the opposite side from what you are used to and driven that car on the opposite side of the road? It takes time and practice before you are comfortable driving in those conditions and you will continue to feel awkward and unsafe for quite some time. With practice, you develop comfort and skill.

> **Authors' Note:** When someone asks such a question in a training session we are conducting, we usually respond with active listening feedback such as, "So the technique seems mechanical to you and you are concerned that others would not like for you to use it with them. Right?" Almost 100% of the time, the person will say "yes" and then elaborate on his concern without realizing that we just used the technique. Often others in the class will notice and may giggle or whisper to someone else about our having just used the technique on their classmate.
>
> We then will explain to the questioner that we just used the technique and that he did not seem to notice. The person acknowledges that he didn't notice and he looks surprised. Then we explain to the class that because we use the technique a lot, we are skillful with it and they, too, can learn to do it well enough that others will not notice and will simply feel understood. The person who questioned the technique is usually relieved after this brief demonstration.

➤ **"Just restating what they say seems to be refusing to help. If you really care, shouldn't you help?"**

Most of us have learned that friends and family members are responsible for helping others solve their problems, and this concern is the one some people struggle with the most. This helps to explain why the most spontaneous response to others who are emotional or baffled by a problem is to start offering suggestions, asking fact-finding questions, telling them what to do, and so on—because we want to help. But these responses have many risks and usually do not help as much as we think they will.

Even if your advice or direction were to result in people's solving their problems, what do they learn about thinking for themselves? The answer is *nothing*.

This is the difference between coaching and *rescuing*. When we rescue people we think for them, we fix it for them, we take the problem and figure out the solution because we think we are helping. What we actually end up doing is robbing them of the opportunity to think for themselves, to learn and grow in self-confidence. We run the risk of training them to become dependent on others rather than learning to take care of themselves.

When you learn to use the active listening paraphrasing technique well enough that it becomes a skill, you experience what a caring thing it is to do for someone. It is a powerful form of positive attention.

CASE STUDY: Paraphrasing Between Friends

Chen and Lester were team leads in a manufacturing company and had been good friends for many years. Lester noticed that Chen seemed to be troubled about something. He seemed to be tired and withdrawn. While having lunch together, Lester asked, "Chen, you look exhausted and seem to be really worried about something. Want to talk about it?"

Chen replied, "Thank you for noticing, Les. Yes, I am really tired. I can't remember when I last had a good night's sleep, but I don't know if talking about it will help anything." Lester answered, "Well buddy, it couldn't hurt, could it? What's going on?"

Sighing deeply, Chen said, "Our oldest son is not doing well in college and told us that he is going to quit. We had such high hopes for him. He would have been the first member of our family to earn a college degree." Les reflected, "Sounds like you are really disappointed about his dropping out of school. Is that it?"

Chen replied, "Well, we are disappointed but mostly we are worried about him. He is a very bright kid and we don't understand why he has done so poorly. We also are concerned about why he did not tell us what was happening until after he had decided to quit." Les responded, "So you are worried about your son and don't really know what has happened. Right?"

"Right. He has always come to us with problems but this was a total surprise. We have tried to get him to talk with us about it but he gets angry and tells us to mind our own business. Les, he is our son and what happens to him is our business." Les looked concerned and asked quietly, "Chen, what do you think you can do?"

Chen looked up and said, "I don't know what to do. What do you think I should do?" Les paused and then said, "You seem to be at a loss about what to do, Chen, and I can tell you are really anxious about what's going on with your boy. Do I have it straight?" Chen sighed again and said, "We've decided that we need to go talk with him face to face because the telephone calls have not worked. We hope that when we see him and hug him and tell him that we love him and will support him no matter what he decides that he will trust us enough to tell us more. I am taking some personal time so we can drive up there to show him we care."

CONTINUED

Les reached out and touched his friend on the shoulder and said, "Chen, that sounds like a really smart plan. I hope it goes well and that all of you will be able to help each other through this situation. I'll be thinking about you and I want to hear all about it later. Okay?"

Chen smiled and said, "Thank you, friend. I wish I had said something to you earlier—it really helped to talk about it with you."

Did Lester ask fact-finding questions?	❑ Yes	❑ No
Did he offer advice?	❑ Yes	❑ No
Did he offer sympathy or reassurance?	❑ Yes	❑ No
Did he seem to care?	❑ Yes	❑ No

Notice that Lester did not use any of the typical responses and did not try to solve his friend's problem, but that he certainly seemed to care. The only question he asked was the open-ended question about what Chen thought he could do. When Chen said that he didn't know what to do and asked his friend what he should do, Lester did not jump in and rescue. By simply acknowledging Chen's uncertainty and anxiety with another active listening restatement, he avoided using any of the usual responses and communicated that he cared.

Did Chen decide what to do about his problem?	❑ Yes	❑ No

We do not know if his attempt to resolve the problem will be successful, but he had already made a decision before Lester even initiated the conversation. Most people do not need to be rescued and they do appreciate being able to confide in a friend or someone they trust and respect. Lester demonstrated genuine concern for his friend and allowed him to talk about what was troubling him. This helped to relieve some of Chen's stress and seemed to strengthen the bond between them.

Coaching Others Through Their Problems

> *When I want to, I perform better than when I have to. I want to for me, I have to for you. Self-motivation is a matter of choice."*
>
> –John Whitmore, *Coaching for Performance*

Determining When to Get Involved in Problem Solving

Sometimes another person may have a problem for which you want or need to play a more active role. To help you determine when to do this, evaluate the nature of the problem by asking a few questions of yourself. For example:

➤ Does the other person have the experience, training, and skills to solve the problem?

➤ Is this a problem that can have a direct impact on me?

➤ Will I be held accountable for the quality of the solution?

If you determine that the other person does not have adequate resources for solving the problem, you may choose to help by providing training, information, or other assistance if it is requested. If the other person has not asked for help and just seems to be frustrated or confused, be careful that you are not stepping into the role of rescuer. This can undermine people's self-confidence and result in their coming to you for help repeatedly.

When the other person's problem has the potential for a direct impact on you, becoming actively involved in finding a solution is appropriate because you are taking care of yourself. But you may still want to give the other person the opportunity to solve the problem on her own to allow her to learn from the experience and to become an independent thinker.

If the problem is one where you are accountable for the outcome, you probably will want to be more involved in determining the solution or at least making sure that the solution is acceptable to you. This is common for work-related problems in which you are the supervisor or manager. But do not just take over. Make certain that your employee plays an active role in solving the problem.

TO GET INVOLVED OR NOT?

The situations that follow will help you understand how to evaluate problems to determine your role in solving them. For each question, check (√) *yes*, *possibly*, or *no* to indicate your answer.

1. **Situation 1:** One of your employees comes to you complaining about how long it takes one of the other team members to complete his part of the multistep process that they work on together. The employee is concerned that you will think he is not doing a good job.

   Is the employee capable of handling this situation on his own?
   ❏ Yes   ❏ Possibly   ❏ No

   Is this a problem that can have a direct impact on me?
   ❏ Yes   ❏ Possibly   ❏ No

   Will I be held accountable for the quality of the solution?
   ❏ Yes   ❏ Possibly   ❏ No

   Will it be best for me to get involved?
   ❏ Yes   ❏ Possibly   ❏ No

2. **Situation 2:** A peer reveals to you during a lunchtime conversation that she is going to start looking for a job in another organization because she is so dissatisfied with her relationship with her boss. She tells you that she is tired of trying to make the relationship work. You know that her leaving will be a serious loss for your organization.

   Is my peer capable of handling this situation on her own?
   ❏ Yes   ❏ Possibly   ❏ No

   Is this a problem that can have a direct impact on me?
   ❏ Yes   ❏ Possibly   ❏ No

   Will I be held accountable for the quality of the solution?
   ❏ Yes   ❏ Possibly   ❏ No

   Will it be best for me to get involved?
   ❏ Yes   ❏ Possibly   ❏ No

CONTINUED

3. **Situation 3:** One of your employees asks if he can work out an arrangement with you for different hours and reveals that he is having some serious problems with a family situation. Your organization does not offer flextime for employees and you inform him that you cannot do what he is asking. He becomes angry on hearing this and says that he will have to seek employment elsewhere.

Is the employee capable of resolving this situation on his own?

❏ Yes ❏ Possibly ❏ No

Is this a problem that can have a direct impact on me?

❏ Yes ❏ Possibly ❏ No

Will I be held accountable for the quality of the solution?

❏ Yes ❏ Possibly ❏ No

Will it be best for me to get involved?

❏ Yes ❏ Possibly ❏ No

4. Now think of a situation in your workplace in which someone wanted you to help solve a problem. Describe the situation on the lines provided and then answer the questions to evaluate whether you should get involved.

The problem: _____

_____

_____

Is the employee capable of resolving this situation on his own?

❏ Yes ❏ Possibly ❏ No

Is this a problem that can have a direct impact on me?

❏ Yes ❏ Possibly ❏ No

Will I be held accountable for the quality of the solution?

❏ Yes ❏ Possibly ❏ No

Will it be best for me to get involved?

❏ Yes ❏ Possibly ❏ No

Compare your answers with those of the authors in the Appendix.

Facilitating a Solution with the Others Involved

When you decide that your active involvement in finding a solution is the right decision, it is important for you to keep the other person(s) involved for several reasons:

➤ People are more committed to making a solution work when it is their own idea

➤ Even when the best solution was not one they thought of, they will have more ownership because they were part of the process

➤ People learn about problem solving by doing it with your aid and gain confidence in their own problem-solving abilities

Three-Step Process

Here is a proven process for facilitating problem solving to involve the other person(s) and to keep you from becoming a rescuer and just taking over.

1. **Focus on the Person as well as the Problem**

   The idea is to help others do their own thinking and to help them learn how to solve problems on their own. Start by giving the others the opportunity to think of solutions for the problem by asking open-ended questions and responding with active listening feedback responses. They may come up with a good solution without your having to suggest any if you are patient and use your listening skills to help them think through the problem.

2. **Offer Information or Ideas and Ask the Others to Evaluate**

   The purpose of asking the others to evaluate the suggestions or information you offer is to keep them thinking and to help them feel that they contributed to the eventual solution. The challenge is to make sure they do not get the impression that you imposed your solution.

3. **Agree Together on the Solution and Implementation**

   Many leaders tend to take charge, make the decision, and assign tasks. The idea with this step is to select a solution together and involve the others in determining the action steps and timing to implement the solution. This will help ensure their feeling of ownership in the process and the solution. Then they will implement the solution with a real commitment to success.

HELPING YOUR EMPLOYEE RESOLVE HIS PROBLEM

The previous exercise described an employee who was concerned that his teammate's slower pace might result in your evaluating his own performance as needing improvement. It is a situation in which you might choose to become involved. As explained in the Appendix for that exercise, you might want to help the employee work with his teammate to resolve the situation without your taking action. Let's say the employee who came to you is José and his teammate is Michelle.

José says to you, "Michelle is so slow finishing her work. I am concerned that you will think I am not working hard because I am waiting for her."

Write an active listening paraphrase (content, feelings, check-out question).

_____

_____

José responds, "Yes. She does a good job, but I get really frustrated when she takes so long."

Now write an active listening paraphrase (content and feelings) and end with an open-ended question asking José how he might do something about the situation.

_____

_____

This time José says, "I don't want her to think I'm telling her how to do her job so I thought it would be better if you said something to her."

Write an active listening response to restate the content, acknowledge his feelings, and follow with a statement about why you think it might be best for José to handle this.

_____

_____

CONTINUED

José replies, "I guess I could offer to help so we can stay on schedule, but she might think I am telling her she is too slow."

Write an active listening response to confirm that you understood his idea and you acknowledge his feelings, and then follow with an open-ended question to ask him how he might reduce the probability of her taking offense to his offer of help.

_____

_____

Compare your work with the authors' responses in the Appendix.

Inducing Changes in Problem Behavior

There will be times when you will be faced with a problem that is the result of another person's unacceptable behavior. When the problem is one that has a direct impact on you, the solution you need is for the behavior to change.

Sometimes you can influence a behavior change by increasing the amount of attention you give to other behaviors. For example, an employee who arrives for work after starting time may be seeking attention. If you tease or reprimand her for her late arrival, this may reinforce the behavior because it does result in her getting attention. Instead, make sure to give her attention on those days when she arrives *on time*—greet her, smile at her, or ask her how she is doing. You may see the late arrivals stop.

When Confrontation Is Called For

If the behavior persists or if the behavior is too potentially costly or unacceptable for other reasons (violates a policy, inappropriate, unsafe, etc.), you will have to deal with it directly and effectively. You will have to confront the problem directly.

Just as an athletic coach has to confront players who violate team rules or who engage in behavior that has a negative impact on their performance, you must take action when an employee's behavior violates the rules, endangers self or others, or affects performance negatively.

Many managers do not confront problem behavior directly because they have not been taught how to do it or they are anxious about how the person might respond. By not confronting, however, they are failing to carry out their responsibility and they are indirectly communicating to the employee that the behavior is not a problem.

Formulating a Caring Confrontation

Confrontation can be difficult because of the possibility of defensive, emotional responses and because most people have not had positive experience with it. The word conjures images of anger, embarrassment, guilt, and conflict because of painful experiences in our past. But confrontation can be done in a caring manner.

Here is a five-part formula to help you prepare:

1. Create Rapport

By making the extra effort to connect with the other person, you improve the likelihood that your discussion will have a positive outcome. You reduce the risk of an extreme reaction when you bring up the subject of changing behavior. Match the other person's style and communicate in that style throughout the discussion.

2. Describe the Behavior

Use words that are factual to describe the other person's behavior. Avoid using words that communicate judgment or blame. You are planning a discussion, not a reprimand.

3. Describe the Effects on You

Explain to the other person how the problem behavior is having an impact on you or how it *could* result in a negative impact on you. This is more effective than talking about "the rules." After all, what do many people think about rules? They are "made to be broken."

By explaining to the person how the behavior is costing *you*, the discussion is personal. That is why it is so effective. People often are not concerned about how their behavior affects a corporation or a government agency, but they typically do not want to be at cross-purposes with a significant person in their lives. As the manager, you are a significant person.

Time, money, productivity, quality, and level of service are examples of potential effects on you as the manager responsible for such things. The most effective impacts are ones that are observable and measurable. These become logical reasons for others to consider changing their behavior.

4. **Tell How You Feel**

By telling the other person how you feel about the impact or potential cost to you, you also humanize the discussion. You are not just talking about profits, costs, and productivity—which can be distant or abstract to the other person—you are talking about how the problem behavior is affecting you emotionally as well as tangibly. That is a powerful message that grabs people's attention and invites them to be accountable for their behavior without coming across as disapproving. It works.

5. **Ask for What You Want**

This is not a time to use commands. Even directing/guiding personality types, who respond positively to being direct and commanding, can react negatively to directives when their behavior is being confronted. Requesting a change will be more effective and is less likely to be perceived as being parental. The other reason to ask is that a request invites a response. You want to get a commitment from the other person. A command is a one-way communication style and a request is a two-way style that asks for a response.

Some options for the request are asking the person to stop the behavior or to start using a different behavior in place of the one being discussed. An important and effective alternative is to ask the other person for a solution. Remember, people are most likely to follow through and make sure it happens when it is their own idea.

ANALYZING THE CARING CONFRONTATION

The situations that follow are examples of the five-part formula for caring confrontation. On the lines provided, identify the elements and the style used in each.

"Elise, I know how much you like your teammates. I am concerned that the several absences you have had in the past few weeks will result in our team's missing our production goals. The others have done a good job of picking up the slack but they can't do it all without you. What will you do to make sure that you are here every day so we all can count on you?"

Personality Style: _____

Behavior: _____

Effect on You: _____

Your Feeling: _____

Request: _____

"Terry, I am really worried about something. Got a minute? The thing that's really bugging me is how you tell me you are going to do something and then you don't do it. That really screws up my schedule and I have to put in extra time to get back on track. Will you *puh-leeze* keep your commitments from now on?"

Personality Style: _____

Behavior: _____

Effect on You: _____

Your Feeling: _____

Request: _____

Compare your answers with the authors' responses in the Appendix.

CONFRONTATION WORKSHEET

Use the situation below to practice identifying the elements and write a few statements. List several effects and the feelings connected with them to give you more to work with. If the person does not respond to one, another one might be more compelling.

Situation:

You have heard complaints from several people in your organization about how one of your employees has been accusatory and angry with them about mistakes or very small problems. Today you actually observed this employee yelling at someone in another department, throwing some papers onto the desk, and accusing the person of intentionally delaying action on his request.

Assume that the person is a directing/guiding personality. Complete the table below and then write your opening statements beneath.

Identify at least three effects and the emotions connected to each. You may also want to consider more than one request.

Personality Style: Directing/Guiding

Behavior	Effect on You	Feeling (emotion)	Request

Your opening statements:

_____

_____

_____

Compare your work with the authors' ideas in the Appendix.

CONFRONTATION IN YOUR WORKPLACE

Think of an employee in your workplace who needs confronting. Again, practice identifying the elements and write a few statements. List several effects and the feelings connected with them to give you more to work with.

Situation:

_____

_____

_____

Assume that the person is an analytical personality. Complete the table below and then write your opening statements beneath.

Identify at least three effects and the emotions connected to each. You may also want to consider more than one request.

Personality Style: Analytical

Behavior	Effect on You	Feeling (emotion)	Request

Your opening statements:

_____

_____

_____

Dealing with Defensive Responses

Even when you prepare thoroughly and use all of your skills to confront people caringly and effectively, there is no guarantee that they will hear what you say and willingly make a commitment to change. Some people have unpleasant memories of being confronted and may have learned to become defensive even when you do it skillfully.

What do you do when others respond defensively? Whether they become angry, or deny that they have behaved the way you described, or break into tears, your most effective response is to use the active listening paraphrasing technique. When you acknowledge their feelings—demonstrating empathy—and prove that you understand by restating what they say, their defensiveness will diminish at least a little.

They were expecting you to retreat or push back and did not expect empathy and understanding, which defuses some of their emotion. They may continue to be defensive several times, but if you respond with empathy and understanding each time, they will eventually return to their normal emotional temperature.

Only when they seem no longer to be defensive do you return to the negotiation in hopes of getting a commitment for change. If you do not defuse their emotional response, they will escalate and you will lose control of the situation.

The graph below shows how it can work.

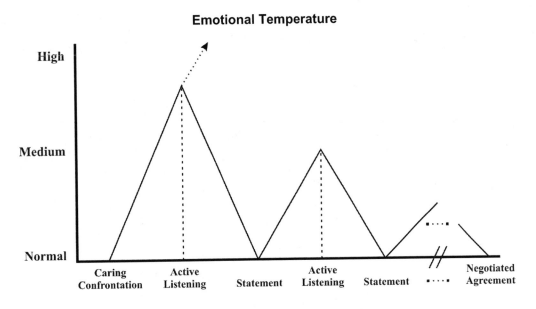

Each time the other person starts getting defensive, you exercise your active listening skills until they calm down. Remember that a single active listening response may not be enough for them to return to normal emotional temperature so be prepared to use several listening responses before continuing to negotiate for a change in behavior. You then continue the discussion in a non-blaming, caring manner with patient persistence until you get a commitment for a change in the behavior.

Investing Time and Energy to Coach Others

Perhaps you are thinking, "But these processes take so long. I don't have time for all of this hand-holding." Yes, they take practice and your first attempts may not succeed. When you have practiced active listening enough, however, that you can do it spontaneously and effectively, the processes do not take as long as they might seem now.

They do take longer than just taking charge, making decisions, and telling others what to do. But the price you pay for doing that is failing to empower people and "training" them to come to you with every little problem rather than acting on their own.

With continued practice, you will find that the coaching approach is very effective and most people will cooperate and change the behavior you have confronted. Most will appreciate your skillful handling of the situation and will respect you for being assertive enough to confront them.

Coaching people through problem solving is making an investment in them. You are investing time and energy in developing people. The dividend this pays you is having employees who are confident, decisive, accountable problem solvers.

A P P E N D I X

Follow-up Suggestions

Many people quickly return to old habits after learning new techniques and ideas. Long-term behavior patterns are strongly ingrained, which is one reason change is challenging. Here are some ideas to help you follow through and implement what you have learned from this book.

Review the book within the next couple of days. If you do not read the book a second time and review your practice exercises, you may forget most of what you learned. People typically forget as much as 70% within a day or two, and within a week or two as much as 90% has been forgotten. Reviewing the book will help you remember and retain as much as 80%.

Practice the techniques. Without practice you cannot become skillful. As valuable as the ideas may be, they are only concepts until you put them to use. They will not become skills or habits without repeated use. Work out a practice schedule rather than trying to use it all at once. Practice different things on different days to keep your goals more achievable and reduce the probability of giving up and going back to old patterns.

Review the book a second time within the next week or 10 days. The second review will help you remember most of what you learned and will remind you of an important thing or two that you had forgotten.

Positive reinforcement is very important for developing skills. Share with others what you are practicing and ask them to give you positive reinforcement when they notice your using what you have learned. Sharing with them what you are doing will also increase the probability of your doing it because you will have put yourself on the line. Knowing that someone is expecting you to improve provides incentive to follow through.

Read more books on related topics. Those on the Additional Reading list at the end of this book will reinforce what you have learned and help you learn more.

Appendix to Part 1

Comments & Suggested Responses

Case Study: Each Learns from Observation

1. Jahnavi realized that the call center representatives did not just talk with customers on the telephone and provide solutions for problems; they also identified causes of the problems that could be changed. By communicating to Rachel that her suggestions for improved service would be appreciated, she opened the door to receiving good suggestions from Rachel that could be applied throughout the call center.

2. Rachel realized that she had misunderstood the importance of one part of her job—making suggestions about what could be improved. Learning that this was an expectation added a new challenge to her job and helped her feel more important in the organization.

3. The company will likely benefit from Rachel having greater job satisfaction, from the improved productivity and/or customer service resulting from her suggestions, and from Jahnavi having learned the value of involving employees. A win-win for all!

Appendix to Part 2

Comments & Suggested Responses

Ways to Give Positive Attention

➤ Smile

➤ Greet

➤ Use their name

➤ Invite to join you (coffee/lunch)

➤ Send a thank-you note

➤ Issue a reward (gift certificate, tickets, etc.)

➤ Ask about family

➤ Ask for their ideas

➤ Use their ideas and give credit

➤ Send a card (birthday, anniversary, etc.)

➤ Give a raise or bonus

➤ Promote them

➤ Give special recognition (e.g., employee of month)

➤ Wave to them

➤ Provide time off

➤ Issue reserved parking

➤ Give a small gift (plant, shirt, mouse pad, etc.)

➤ Pay for association dues, conference

➤ Listen skillfully

Is This Good Feedback?

1. Poor—Judgment rather than factual description; suggestion was helpful

2. Good—Specific factual description of behavior

3. Good—Specific factual description of behavior

4. Poor—Hearsay; no behavior defined (attitude is not observable)

5. Fair—Mentions work but provides judgment rather than specific feedback (if the work is only a little above average it should not be rated as good)

6. Good—Specific factual description of behavior

What Would You Say?

1. Maria, thank you for completing the PowerPoint presentation early. I appreciate having the extra time for practice and I really like the creative graphics. As always, it was error free. Very nice job.

2. Thank you for facilitating the session today, Sayeed. I noticed that you interrupted people when they attempted to offer suggestions and told them that the purpose of the session was to define the objectives. Even though this was true, people did not respond positively to the interruptions and they seemed to withdraw from participating. How could you have handled the meeting differently to keep them more involved?

3. Well, Phillipe, your first assignment is done. How do you think it went? (Pause for response.) I think the quality of your work was fine, particularly considering that it was your first project. You took a little longer than I thought you would. How do you feel about the timing?

4. Kathleen, I have some concern about your correcting people in front of the other team members and speaking harshly to them when they do not quickly understand your instructions. How can you handle these situations in the future to be more supportive with your team to help build their confidence and trust in you?

Matching Feedback to Personality

1. Supporting/Caring
2. Directing/Guiding
3. Expressive
4. Supporting/Caring
5. Analytical
6. Expressive
7. Analytical
8. Directing/Guiding
9. Supporting/Caring
10. Directing/Guiding

Giving Feedback in Different Styles

Situation 1

Directing/Guiding style:

You nailed it, Lynn! Completing your project on time was key for rolling out the new line for the peak season. Good job.

Analytical style:

Excellent work on the project, Lynn. Your planning and execution were thorough and on schedule. This new line being available for the peak season was a key objective and your leadership is appreciated.

Supporting/Caring style:

You came through for us, Lynn. Thank you very much for helping to get our new line ready for the peak season. I knew I could depend on you.

Expressive style:

Super job, Lynn! Getting our new line out there for the peak season will make a real splash! You're the greatest!

Situation 2

Directing/ Guiding style:

Robin, there has been a noticeable drop in the number of orders being processed in the past few weeks. Help me understand what has happened.

Analytical style:

Robin, when I was examining the weekly reports I noticed a decrease in the number of orders being processed during the past three weeks. Will you give me your analysis of the cause?

Supporting/Caring style:

Robin, I am concerned about the recent drop in the number of orders being processed. I hope that you are okay. (Pause.) Will you please help me understand what has caused this?

Expressive style:

Hey, Robin. How you doin'? I noticed that we're getting fewer orders processed recently and that's kind of scary. What's happening?

Appendix to Part 3

Comments & Suggested Responses

What Is a Good Learning Objective?

1. Poor—Knowing how to do something is not enough. A better objective would be to handle an irate customer successfully. It would be important to define the criteria for what is considered to be successful.

2. Good—Defines specifically what the learner will be able to do.

3. Good—Defines specifically what the learner will be able to do.

4. Good—Defines specifically what the learner will be able to do.

5. Fair—Describes behavior but does not specify quality standards.

6 Poor—Vague expectation of learning about something, not learning how to do something.

Case Study: A Team Meeting

Courtney is *visual*. She uses a visual presentation and uses visual referents when speaking. She also asked Kevin for a copy of his notes.

Beth is *auditory*. She asked about what Courtney said rather than what she saw on the screen, and she used auditory words.

Kevin is *visual*. Even though Kevin was listening to Beth before the meeting started, his most consistent style was visual as evidenced by using his computer to take notes, offering to send copies to everyone, asking about what he saw on the screen, and using visual referents in his speech.

Donovan is *kinesthetic*. He was moving a lot before the meeting began, smacked the table with his hand, and used action words repeatedly.

Case Study: Stacy Learns from Her Mistake

1.   Stacy, that seemed to be a tough call. Are you okay?

2.   I remember a similar situation when I was trying to help a customer. He was talking so fast and was so angry that I just could not understand the problem. I eventually lost it and told him to buy a "Computers for Dummies" book!

3.   Stacy, what did you say to that customer that could have been done better?

    Well, what I heard you say was "you are not making any sense." How do you think that invited the customer to feel?

4.   How can you fix this situation? (Pause – listen.) That's a good idea, Stacy. People usually appreciate an apology and the free upgrade might demonstrate good faith on our part, particularly if you are able to figure out the problem and resolve it.

5.   How will you respond the next time you have a customer who is struggling to explain a problem to you?

Appendix to Part 4

Comments & Suggested Responses

Recognizing the Risks of Some Responses

1. **Telling, Commanding**

   Many people do not like to be told what to do and they will react defensively. If that does not happen and the other person does what you told him to do, he may blame you if the outcome is not acceptable. If the outcome is acceptable, he may expect you to guide him in the future and may become dependent on you.

2. **Asking Questions**

   If the person answers your question, she will be talking about whatever you asked about and this can be a diversion from what she intended to communicate. If you do this several times, she may become frustrated. Even if your questions help to define the situation more clearly and facilitate finding a solution, you are doing most of the thinking and the person may expect you to do that in the future as mentioned above.

   Closed questions are those that can be answered either yes or no or with a one-word response. This tends to shut down communication and you have to ask many questions to learn anything. Plus, you are determining the subject rather than allowing the person to talk about what she wishes to discuss.

3. **Offering Suggestions or Help**

   People often do not want advice from others and they tend to reject suggestions by finding fault with them. You and the other person may become frustrated with this process. If he acts on your advice, you have the same risks as explained above—blaming you for bad advice or depending on you in the future.

   Offering help can result in your taking some unnecessary ownership in the problem or situation and you may later regret becoming involved.

4. **Reassuring, Encouraging**

   Even though most people have learned to do this, it can sound patronizing to the other person and she may resent it. Even if your words do help her feel better, you may have reinforced her taking no action, which interferes with resolving a problem. It may also reinforce a pattern of passivity. Guess what she will do the next time she feels bad? Come looking for you to help her feel better.

5. **Preaching, Moralizing, Pushing Beliefs**

   This response often will trigger an argument and bad feelings. If the person does not object to your applying your values and standards to him and his situation, he may later blame you for leading him astray or seek you out when he has another problem.

6. **Explaining, Giving Logical Reasons**

   This can sound uncaring to many people and may even be heard as patronizing or condescending. If there is no negative reaction, the person may understand better as a result of your explanation but she learns nothing about thinking for herself. She may become dependent on your explaining things for her.

7. **Using Humor, Sidetracking, or Withdrawing**

   Often a symptom of our own discomfort, this can signal to the other person that you don't care or are not taking him seriously, which can result in bad feelings toward you. If used repeatedly, this response can damage your relationship (as can the other responses).

8. **Agreeing, Taking Their Side**

   If you agree or tell the person that she is right, she may choose to do something that she regrets and she may blame you. Somewhat like encouraging or reassuring, this can be heard as insincere or a brush-off.

9. **Apologizing**

   Most of us are quick to apologize if the other person is upset about something we did. But the apology may not be heard as sincere or sufficient. Often people apologize even when they have done nothing wrong and this reinforces taking responsibility for the feelings of others, which can contribute to relationship problems. Apology often will do little to defuse the other person's emotions.

10. **Criticizing, Disapproving, Judging**

    This response will usually invite the other person to react defensively and emotionally. Not only can this result in conflict, it may damage a relationship.

Acknowledge Others' Feelings

1. "You sound pretty frustrated with that document. Hard to understand, huh?"

2. "Kind of scary being the new guy when layoffs are being considered, isn't it?"

3. "Boy, you're pretty fed up with Gunther. Right?"

4. "Oops. You sound pretty discouraged about your problems with the worksheet. Am I right?"

5. "Sounds like all of the meetings are interfering with your work and you seem unhappy about that. Is that what you're saying?"

Appendix to Part 5

Comments & Suggested Responses

To Get Involved or Not?

1. **Situation 1**

    Is the employee capable of handling this situation on his own?

    ☑ Yes   ☐ Possibly   ☐ No

    Is this a problem that can have a direct impact on you?

    ☑ Yes   ☐ Possibly   ☐ No

    Will you be held accountable for the quality of the solution?

    ☐ Yes   ☑ Possibly   ☐ No

    Will it be best for you to get involved?

    ☐ Yes   ☐ Possibly   ☑ No

    When your employees have difficulties with each other, it is tempting to step in, but the best resolution will probably be one that they work out together. It would be appropriate for you to express concern about the situation and to use your active listening and coaching skills to help the employee think of alternatives for improving the relationship with the co-worker. Open-ended questions could help the complaining employee realize that the quality of the work is important. If timing is a concern, open-ended questions could also help to communicate with the other employee about that. You may decide that a little on-the-spot teaching would help the employee learn to communicate more effectively with the other.

2. **Situation 2**

   Is the employee capable of handling this situation on her own?

   ☑ Yes   ☐ Possibly   ☐ No

   Is this a problem that can have a direct impact on me?

   ☐ Yes   ☑ Possibly   ☐ No

   Will I be held accountable for the quality of the solution?

   ☐ Yes   ☐ Possibly   ☑ No

   Will it be best for me to get involved?

   ☐ Yes   ☑ Possibly   ☐ No

   Even though this person's leaving would have a negative impact on your organization, it is her decision to make and she is capable of making it. If her departure would have a negative impact on your ability to perform, then it could be a situation in which you have some concern about her decision. It still might not justify your becoming involved in an attempt to persuade her to stay.

3. **Situation 3**

Is the employee capable of handling this situation on his own?

☐ Yes   ☑ Possibly   ☐ No

Is this a problem that can have a direct impact on me?

☑ Yes   ☐ Possibly   ☐ No

Will I be held accountable for the quality of the solution?

☐ Yes   ☑ Possibly   ☐ No

Will it be best for me to get involved?

☑ Yes   ☐ Possibly   ☐ No

Because your employee's productivity will be affected by his family problems and he may even leave your organization, you have a need to be involved in working with him to find a solution. Because the problem is something that is outside of the workplace, your involvement will be restricted to alternatives that are work-related.

By using your active listening skills to demonstrate empathy and understanding and giving the employee an opportunity to talk about what is troubling him, you may learn more about his problem. Together you can seek workplace alternatives besides the flextime solution he requested. He may be unaware of your employee assistance program and how to use it. You may be able to arrange a flexible schedule by asking for authorization even though your organization does not have an existing policy.

If you had responded with active listening immediately, the employee probably would not have become angry and threatened to quit, but you can start using the skills at this point to salvage the situation.

Helping Your Employee Resolve His Problem

"I want to be sure I am understanding, Jose. You sound frustrated with Michelle because of her timing and you're concerned that it will affect my evaluation of your performance. Right?"

"So you're telling me that she does good work and it is just how long she takes that bothers you. What can you do about this?"

"Okay, because you're concerned that if you say something to her about the time issue, she will think that you are being bossy and this is the reason you've come to me. True?" [Jose says yes.] "I am concerned that if I get involved, she will be upset with you for coming to me instead of speaking with her yourself. When the boss is involved, it seems to make it a big deal and the two of you might be able to resolve this without me. How might you work with her to improve the situation?"

"Uh-huh. One possibility would be for you to offer to help her so the work could be finished more quickly, but you are worried that she might take your offer as telling her she's too slow. Right? [Jose confirms.] "How might you make the offer in a way that she would be less likely to get that impression?"

Analyzing the Caring Confrontation

Elise situation

Personality Style:	Supporting/Caring
Behavior:	Several absences
Effect on You:	Reduced productivity and overloading team members (The reason for talking about the impact on the team is to match what a supporting/caring person values more than anything else—relationships.)
Your Feeling:	Concerned
Request:	Solution and a commitment

Terry situation

Personality Style:	Expressive
Behavior:	Not keeping commitments
Effect on You:	Have to reschedule and put in extra time
Your Feeling:	Bugging you (matching "feeling" word choice with expressive style)
Request:	Keep commitments

Confrontation Worksheet

Behavior	Effect on You	Feeling (emotion)	Request
Yelling	Employees who receive this treatment will be stressed—affects their productivity	Concerned	Manage emotions
Throwing papers		Worried	Be respectful with others
Accusing		Fearful	Suggested solution
	Others may retaliate by refusing to cooperate—affects productivity	Concerned	
		Disappointed in this person's behavior	
	Productivity problems may result in criticism of my performance as the manager		
	Possible lawsuit for hostile work environment		

Confrontation Statements:

"[Name], please tell me about that situation I observed a short while ago when I saw you yelling at [Name]."

(Remember to use active listening feedback responses several times if necessary to help lower the other person's emotional temperature before continuing to work toward an agreement.)

"I have heard complaints from several people about your treating them in that manner and I was disappointed to see you doing that. I am also worried that such treatment will have a negative impact on morale and productivity."

(Remember to use active listening feedback responses several times if necessary to help lower the other person's emotional temperature before continuing to work toward an agreement.)

"[Name], it is important that we treat one another respectfully if we are going to function as an effective, productive team. How will you handle situations in the future?"

Additional Reading

Alessandra, Tony, and Michael O'Connor. *People Smarts*. NY: Pfeiffer, 1994.

Bonet, Diana. *The Business of Listening, Third Edition*. Crisp Series, 2001.

Braham, Barb, and Janice Berry. *Retaining Your Employees*. Crisp Series, 2001.

Daniels, Aubrey C. *Bringing Out the Best in People*. NY: McGraw-Hill, 2000.

Finch, Lloyd. *Delegation Skills for Leaders, Third Edition*. Crisp Series, 2005.

Fournies, Ferdinand F. *Coaching for Improved Work Performance*. NY: McGraw-Hill, 2000.

Hathaway, Patti. *Feedback Skills for Leaders, Third Edition*. Crisp Series, 2005.

Kouzes, James, and Barry Posner. *The Leadership Challenge*. NY: Jossey-Bass, 1996.

LaBorde, Genie Z. *Influencing with Integrity*. Palo Alto, CA: Syntony, 1983.

LeBoeuf, Michael. *The Greatest Management Principle in the World*. NY: Berkley, 1985.

Lloyd, Sam R. *Accountability*: *Managing for Maximum Results*. Crisp Series, 2002.

Lloyd, Sam R. *Developing Positive Assertiveness, Third Edition*. Crisp Series, 2002.

Minor, Marianne. *Coaching & Counseling, Third Edition*. Crisp Series, 2002.

Whitmore, John. *Coaching for Performance: Growing People, Performance and Purpose*. London: Brealey, Nicholas Publishing, 2002.

Zuker, Elaina. *Creating Rapport, Revised Edition*. Crisp Series, 2005.

NOTES

NOTES

NOTES

NOTES

NOTES

Also Available

Books • Videos • CD-ROMs • Computer-Based Training Products

If you enjoyed this book, we have great news for you. There are more than 200 books available in the *Crisp Fifty-Minute™ Series*. For more information visit us online at

www.courseilt.com

Subject Areas Include:

Management

Human Resources

Communication Skills

Personal Development

Sales/Marketing

Finance

Coaching and Mentoring

Customer Service/Quality

Small Business and Entrepreneurship

Training

Life Planning

Writing

VERP